top fives

nottingham 2002

So what's new in Nottingham? Well possibly you are. Whether you're here on business or pleasure, if you're a flash git who's just moved into any of the new city centre residential developments, or you're one of the tens of thousands of new students in the city, we're here to help steer you in the right direction.

Even if you're not a newcomer to Nottingham it's pretty taxing keeping up to date with all the developments, and with all the new people in the city we obviously need a whole load of new places to spend our cash. You can be pretty sure that any centrally located building that hasn't been converted into loft style apartments is now a fancy bar/restaurant, and there's also been a fair few shake-ups to the shopping scene.

La Tasca

But what if you're not a loft-dwelling, bar loafer? Don't panic. In the line of duty, we at itchy are not adverse to dining on dodgy kebabs and cheap curries or seeking out the best happy hours to save you a quid or two. In fact, whatever your bag is, from nu-metal to nouvelle cuisine we've got the low down for you.

Bars, clubs, restaurants and people aren't the only new things in town. The whole landscape of the city is changing. Just as we're getting used to the Ice Centre, new developments like the Cornerhouse are springing up to dominate the skyline, and even the long awaited tram is starting to take shape. All in all, Nottingham is keeping on its toes, staying one step ahead of the pack, and retaining its title as one of the coolest cities in the country. The city itself is really compact, with the distinct areas of the Lace Market, Hockley, and Market Square all within easy walking distance. Moving out of the centre, there's the student areas of Lenton and the Arboretum, the middle class suburbia of West Bridgford, and the war zones of the Meadows and Saint Annes.

Two Hours in Nottingham

An essential calling point on a flying visit to the city would have to be Nottingham Castle. Centrally located, impeccably maintained and providing some stunning views of the truly bizarre Inland Revenue building; it's definitely worth the effort. The immediate vicinity of the castle also encapsulates most of what the city is famous for, from the Lace Museum and the underground caves to the Robin Hood statue. This whistle stop history tour will conveniently leave you with enough time for a crafty pint or two, and where better to quench your thirst than at the handily placed Olde Trip to Jerusalem, (reportedly the oldest pub in England.)

Two Days in Nottingham

The ultimate weekender

Stay – at The Lace Market Hotel, at £60-80 pounds a night it may not be the priciest in the city but it's got a bit more personality than most and it's handy for town.

Shop – seeing as we're on a blow out, it's got to be Bridlesmith Gate for some new threads. There's plenty of places to spunk your wedge but for the guys, Paul Smith should be compulsory – treat yourself to a suit and you'll be ready for some serious bar-hopping later on. And for the girls, you really shouldn't miss Milli, Reiss or Jigsaw.

Paul Smith

Attractions – I suppose you're obliged to head out to Sherwood Forest, although my advice would be to just walk up to the Arboretum and pretend you're in Robin Hood country.

Eat – this is where you'll feel the benefit of all that pre-planning, as you've booked yourself a table at Harts haven't you. No? World Service? OK if it's short notice you could certainly do worse than Wok Wok or La Tasca.

Drink – if you're around the castle area then the automatic place for your post dinner drinks has to be Escape. Then it's time to head to the poseur's paradise of the Lace Market. The calling points on the way are Casa and Fashion, but once there, take your pick from Brass Monkey, Sugar Bar, or Bluu.

Club – your natural course should now take you to the The Lizard Lounge but if you want to drop your guard for a short while then Bar None is a more casual alternative.

Nottingham on the cheap

A bargainous weekend for less than £100.

Stay – fall out of the train station and straight into the Bentink Hotel. (£19, sorted.)

Shop – it's time to prioritise. New clobber is out of the question but Selectadisc may well have that rare Strokes 7" promo you've been looking for. (£5)

Attractions – entertaining as they are, the Caves of Nottingham, Galleries of Justice and Tales of Robin Hood all cost cash, so it's a quick scoot around the Castle and the Lace Museum. (£0)

Eat – you've got to treat yourself to at least one decent meal even if you are watching the pennies, and City Spice is much more affordable than it looks or tastes. Some chain pubs like Hogshead do the odd good offer so you can give the old beans on toast a wide berth for the weekend. (£25)

Drink – there are permanently cheap boozers and low-end options along Upper Parliament Street, but if you're really clever you can hit the happy hours at some of the classier places like Bar Risa without getting stung. (£30)

Club – get camped in The Works early enough and you avoid any door tax, and that of course also applies to late bars like The Social which isn't too steep at the bar either.(£20)

Total Cost – £99.

£1 left. Anybody fancy a hot-dog?

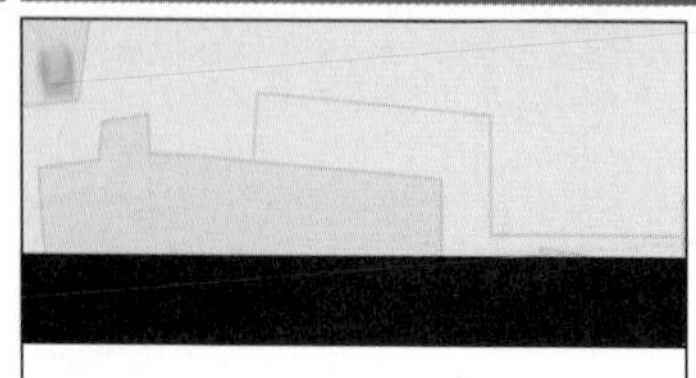

restaurants

www.itchynottingham.co.uk

American

Hooters

Great Northern Close, London Road
(0115) 958 8111

An American tradition for over 15 years, this London Road outlet still stands as the only Hooters restaurant in England. With a quirky sense of humour reflected in the menu, this alternative take on the traditional American diner offers simple and tasty American food served to you at your table by the famous Hooter Girls. If that wasn't incentive enough (and let's face it, it should be) there's also big screen action to watch all the major sporting events, and we're not just talking about the Super Bowl and the World Series but 'proper' football, rugby, and just about anything worth watching over a few pitchers of beer. Popular for business lunches throughout the week, and with livelier groups in the evenings, it takes on a more family oriented feel on Sundays when kids eat for free.

Mon-Thu 12-12, Fri-Sat 11.30-2am, Sun 12pm-10.30

Meal for two: £21 (Philly cheese steak)

British

Escape

5-7 Castle Road (0115) 947 3355

A deceptively large restaurant situated on the first floor above the Escape bar that stands at the foot of Nottingham Castle. It offers a good selection of mostly English food ranging from up-market pub grub to some fancier main dishes.

Mon-Sat 12-11

Meal for 2 £30 (Seared scallops)

Harry Ramsden's

Riverside Park, Queens Drive
(0115) 986 1304

The World's most famous, the biggest, the best... with all the decent fish & chip shops being up North (I'm sorry Midlanders, but its true), Harry Ramsden's comes to the rescue and saves Nottingham's lagging F'n'C scene. With such variations on the menu as Cod & Chips, Haddock & Chips, Chips with Cod, Chips with Haddock, Haddock & Chips with Bap, Chips with Haddock and Peas, Cod, you can tell, the options are endless. Maybe not, but it serves up exactly what you'd expect, with no pretence.

Sun-Thu 10-9.30pm, Fri-Sat 10am-10.30pm

Meal for two: £19.50 (Cod & Chips)

Harts

Standard Court, Park Row
(0115) 911 0666

Widely regarded as the yardstick by which Nottingham's restaurants are measured, Harts offers superb food and excellent pres-

entation in a warm gallery atmosphere. Many places can go overboard with the presentation but few can match Harts for innovative and tasty food. The menu changes daily, but dishes of the likes of roasted scallops and saffron risotto or wood pigeon tartlette are fairly typical. As you'd expect, this is one of the more expensive restaurants in town but you certainly get what you pay for, or, (preferably), what you can get someone else to pay for.

Mon-Sat 12-2 and 7-10.30. Sun 12-2 and 7-9

Meal for two: £41.50 (Three course Sunday menu)

East Asian

Hanson

2 Carrington Street (0115) 950 6615

'Chinese food kills you!', claimed the front-page headline of a popular British tabloid newspaper in summer 2001. Nice work you monkeys – another piece of supreme investigative journalism obviously prompted by a quiet newsday (perhaps Dane Bowers was on holiday, unable to tell us all yet again about how he dumped Jordan). Besides, it was brilliant research - millennia of eating egg fried rice and sweet and sour pork has clearly stunted the population growth of the people of China hasn't it? There's only about 2 billion of them. Those who dare brave the dangers of soy sauce, which will be anyone with half a brain, could do worse than heading here for some agreeable Chinese food in reasonably pleasant surroundings. Those impressed by the dim sum delights can always nip downstairs to the Chinese supermarket, buy up all the ingredients, rush home, get the wok out and rustle up something that tastes not even remotely similar. D'oh.

Mon-Thu 12-10.30, Fri-Sat 12-11.30, Sun 12-9.30
Meal for two: £41.50 (Vegetarian banquet)

Mandarin

23 Hockley (0115) 958 6037

Sorry, is it me? I don't know whether I'm a walking affront to Chinese restaurant protocol but there's never a hint of sweetness on the sour faces of the staff here. You'd think my cack-handed ineptitude would be likely to raise a smile from 10th Dan chopstick masters, but you'd be wrong. They always look like someone's shat in their chop suey to me. So, we've established people don't come here for the hospitality, but thankfully the food itself is a major improvement, and I have to concede it's amongst the best in town. Highly authentic and top notch, it more than makes up for the funeral atmos-

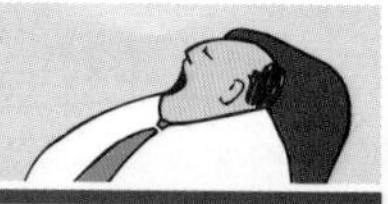

phere and besides, who wants to be fawned over when they're eating anyway?
Mon-Sat 12-2.30, 6-12, Sun 12-10
Meal for two: £23.50 (Fried squid and salted mustard greens)

Siam Thani
16-20a Carlton Street (0115) 958 2222
Slightly bigger than first impression may suggest, this 150 seater L-shaped Thai restaurant is perfectly equipped to cater for large parties. Whilst Nottingham is actually pretty well blessed for decent Thai restaurants this is probably my favourite (although there's not a lot in it). With a hint of Chinese cuisine and some overtones of Indian cooking the advantage it holds over those established favourites is that whilst it leaves you more sated than a sweet and sour, it's not as gut busting as a full-on Balti. Thai food can be a bit fiery, but that's just a perfect excuse for downing more bottles of Chang beer really.
Mon-Sat 12-3pm, 6pm-11pm, Sun 6-11pm
Meal for two: £22.50 (Ped Makam sweet and sour grilled duck)

Skinny Sumo
11-13 Carlton Street, Hockley (0115) 955 1032
"Excuse me, uh, I don't think this is cooked properly". Actually this 'sushi' restaurant isn't exclusively dedicated to raw fish and seaweed as there's plenty of rice and noodle based dishes if you're not feeling too adventurous. Modern and minimal in a contemporary Japanese style it actually feels somewhat intimidating and it might be advisable to take someone who professes to know what they're doing on your visit, if only to laugh at them when they use the finger-dips as an ashtray.
Meal for two: £22 (Beef with Udon Noodles)

Wagamama
The Cornerhouse (0115 9241797)

Taking a modern approach on traditional Japanese noodle bars, Wagamama strips the dining experiences down to the basics. The décor is clean and minimal and bathed in light from the floor-to-ceiling windows. The food is similarly basic with traditional Japanese noodle, rice, and curry dishes presented with the minimum of fuss. The rows of picnic bench-like tables can't be reserved, so it's a case of queuing up by the exposed kitchen area (and even out of the door when it's busy) and waiting your turn. All your orders are hand written onto your paper placemats whilst being automatically radioed through to the kitchen, and to ensure that your food reaches you in prime condition it's all prepared freshly and dispatched to your table the instant it's ready. This can lead to dishes arriving at your table at intervals, especially for larger parties, so there's no standing on ceremony, just crack into it, and fight off anyone trying to get their chopsticks round your teppan fried noodles. This up-market fast food ethic might not be to the taste of those expecting a traditional British dining experience, but it's definitely a welcome addition to Nottingham's restaurant scene for most. The clientele may be predominantly trendy young types, but the surprisingly generous servings ensure that Wagamama is also good enough value to attract a fair few students and anyone looking for a bit of fine dining on a budget.

Mon-Sat 12-11 Sun 12.30-10
Meal for two: £19 (Yaki Soba - noodles with chicken, shrimp, and peppers)

Wok Wok

15 St Peters Gate (0115) 958 8472

After its recent refurb Wok Wok restaurant is once again as fresh and light as the food it serves. Part of a growing national chain it may be, but it comes highly recommended as the food is very authentic and very enjoyable whether you opt for one of the Malaysian curries or a Singapore noodle dish. A couple of the South East Asian dishes on the menu may necessitate easy access to a plentiful supply of soothing iced water, but on the whole the food is very delicate in its fusion of flavours and pleasantly presented with a minimum of fuss.

Mon-Thu 12-10, Fri-Sat 12-11, Sun 12-9.30
Meal for two: £22.50 (Chicken Laksa)

Indian

City Spice

itchy Card 2002

7-9 Thurland Street (0115) 941 2629

If you search around you'll probably find posher (and pricier) Indian restaurants in Nottingham, but you're unlikely to find one much better. City Spice is definitely one of the best curry houses in town and is very competitively priced given the smart and modern feel of the place.

Mon-Sat 6-12.30
Meal for two: £23.50 (Chicken Karahi)

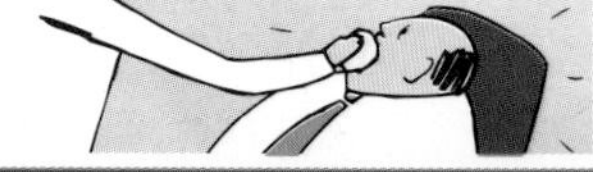

Laguna Tandoori

43 Mount Street (0115) 941 1632

Low-profile Indian restaurant hidden away off Maid Marion Way, the Laguna has survived for years and years thanks to word of mouth. And the word is pretty good. Regarded by many as the best in town, it's noted for its distinctive Tandor oven cooking and many of the regulars will tell you they just won't eat Indian anywhere else. It's not all trendy and posh like some newer curry houses but it's certainly not cheap either, though most agree it's well worth it.

Mon-Sat 6-12am
Meal for two: £22 (Chicken chaat)

Sapna Restaurant

16 St James Street (0115) 941 1026

'If you want to eat, eat. If you want to be cheeky, get out' was the instruction on our last visit. Being a curry house that caters specifically for the after-pub crowd clearly does nothing for their disposition. Understandable really when your clientele is mostly made up of groups of pissed-up revellers demanding 'The hottest curry you do' and washing it down with half a dozen bottles of Cobra.

Mon-Sat 7pm-2am, Sun 7pm-12am
Meal for two: £22 (Lamb bhuna)

Shimla Pink

38-46 Goose Gate (0115) 958 9899

Opened in 1999 to a hail of publicity and attention, Shimlas seemed destined to revolutionise Indian dining in the city. With frosted glass windows, marble tiled floor and modern light interior it certainly challenged a few stereotypes. A couple of years down the line though, and many people are wondering if it was just a case of all style and no substance. General consensus would suggest that standards have fallen along with the size of the portions. One thing that hasn't dropped however is the salt content level of most of the dishes, which is perhaps a management ploy to encourage the punters into exaggerated levels of beer consumption. It's still an impressive place and the food certainly isn't terrible, but the real connoisseurs might be better served elsewhere.

Mon-Fri 11-3, 6-11, Fri-Sat 6-11pm
Meal for two: £28 (Chicken tikka saag)

Shabab Nan Kebab

6 Radford Road, Hyson Green
(0115) 978 1696

In the hope of avoiding an international incident I shall apologise at this point for including this Pakistani restaurant in the Indian section, it's just that it's the only restaurant, to my knowledge, of its type in Nottingham. Whether through ignorance or not, Pakistani food is very much lumped in with it's sub-continental neighbour, and to my uncultured palette it's not a million miles away in terms of taste. One thing that does single out Shabab Nan Kebab is the value for money. A proper decent feed for about a fiver can't be knocked and while it's hardly Kublai Khan's stately pleasure dome, it's certainly not a dump either.

Mon-Sat 6-12

Meal for two: £20 (Chicken curry)

Italian

Caffé Uno

8 Low Pavement (0115) 958 5780

One of Caffé Uno's strongest points has to be the atmosphere of the place. If you're calling in for a bit of lunch between circuiting the near-by fashion houses or making a night of it at the weekend it never disappoints with its friendly and welcoming vibe. Of course the bottom line is the food, and people clearly wouldn't enjoy themselves as much here as they evidently do if the Italian cuisine wasn't up to scratch.

Mon-Sun 12-11pm

Meal for two: £30 (Pollo a masala)

California Pizza Factory

20 Victoria Street (0115) 985 9955

Woah. Like, who totally squashed my dinner dude? No I don't get the Californian connection either. I can only presume it's some way of justifying some rather unconventional pizza toppings, although what West Coast beach bums would make of the full English, (complete with bacon and eggs) I wouldn't like to think. Purists may well baulk at a menu that offers Peking duck pizzas next to pasta based Thai dishes, but it could be argued that the eclectic nature of what's on offer means there's something for every taste, and the food itself really isn't too bad at all.

Mon-Sun 12-11pm

Meal for two: £23 (Traditional English breakfast pizza)

Melinda, 19, Canadian

Your interests are...
Reading, writing, meeting people.
Favourite place for a drink?
Pitcher and Piano
Ha! Doesn't take much does it! How about restaurant?
Petit Paris
Favourite shop so far?
I haven't bought anything yet.
Disgraceful. How about for a club?
I've only been to Faces, and it was crap.
What do you like about Nottingham?
Everybody is up-front and straight talking
And what don't you?
It might all be bullshit

Da Vinci's

70 Bridgeford Road, West Bridgeford (0115) 981 1419

The thing I love most about this place is that you feel you're walking into someone's front room. The decor is minimal, lamps and candles are used for lighting and the music is so subtle, you barely realise you're hearing it. Looking at the menu, it comes as a real surprise that this is a 'no frills' kind of place. The staff are friendly and informal and for a pretty posh place, there's none of that pulling your chair out or positioning your napkin stuff. The food is distinctly Italian but there's more than just pizza and pasta. The prices fall within the medium range (£9-£12 for main course) but once you've tasted the food, you'll think that's damned good value. Starters such as crab and spinach salad or goats cheese soufflé come highly recommended, as does the spinach and ricotta tart or the salmon for main. The selection is good for veggies too; they have two meat, two fish and two vegetable options on the main course. The menu is quite select but changes every two weeks to maintain variety. Overall this is a chilled out place to have a fine dinner - but do book as they get pretty busy at the weekend.

Mon-Sat 12pm-3pm and 7pm-10.30pm.

Sun 12pm-3pm

Meal for two: £28 (Pasta rissotto)

Pizza Express

24-26 Goose Gate (0115) 912 7888

They might be an ever-expanding chain but they generally do things with a modicum of style, and this Hockley outlet continues the trend. Very pleasant, airy and slap-bang in a prime location, (which makes it odd that it's not as busy as its perpetually rammed sister restaurant on King Street). Consequently the vibe is a bit more relaxed, but that's no bad thing, as you can while away the hours with a few carafes of Chianti before heading on to any of the nearby bars, (which are a big improvement on the majority around the other restaurant.) The pizzas themselves are pretty good (although a few more olives wouldn't go amiss), and while the other dishes may not be the most authentic, they're more than acceptable.

Mon-Sat 12-12, Sun 12-10.30

Meal for two: £25 (American Hot pizza)

La Vecchio Romagno

Derby Road (0115 941 9443)

A safety-conscious approach is taken to create a romantic ambience in this longstanding traditional Italian with ingeniously flickering light bulbs substituting for those dangerous candle things. Hmm, what a relief. 'Glockenspiel Moods' and 'Tinky Winky plays the Classics' may be curious selections for the background music, but if you can put up with monotonous plinking and plonking without going crazy, you should find your food highly enjoyable. Reasonably priced and highly authentic, the quality of the food ensures that there's a steady flow of people prepared to risk their sanity.

Mon-Sat 6-11

Meal for two: £27.50 (Cannoloni)

top 5 for...
eats to impress

1. Harts
2. World Service
3. Petit Paris
4. Bentons
5. Escape

Zizzi

10 King Street (0115) 950 9654

Italians don't have a great track record in Nottingham (just ask David Platt) and this latest arrival does little to buck that trend. It looks the part, stylish and suave like an Italian playboy, but a closer inspection reveals it to be all fake tan and imitation Armani. Bland, cold pasta with straight-from the-jar tasting sauces may pass the taste test for a table full of pissed-up bank clerks but I doubt it will impress many others. The pizzas may be a massive improvement but this level of laziness is just not cool. Don't be fooled by appearances, Zizzi looks set to establish itself as the Andrea Silenzi of the Nottingham tratorria scene.

Mon-Sat 11-11, Sun 12-10.30pm

Meal for two: £23.50 (Meatballs)

French

The Dome

13 St Peters Gate (0115) 979 9995

Zut Alors!' was once the cry when hit with your drinks bill in here. But thankfully the days of the most expensive Stella in town are long gone, making it a far more appealing place to call in. Couple the sensible drinks prices with a fixed-price menu and you can wind up having a decent feed in rather refined surroundings for under a tenner.

Mon 11-10, Tues-Fri 11-10.30, Sat 9am-10.30pm, Sun 9am-10pm

Meal for two: £25 (Tuna steak nicoise)

Petit Paris

Kings Walk (0115) 947 3767

Hidden away on Kings Walk, and with the most under-whelming of frontages, you'd think this French restaurant would be easily missed. Well, clearly a large proportion of Nottingham's Francophiles have deemed it worthy of seeking out, as it's consistently busy. The enduring popularity, coupled with the petit (sorry) layout means you need to book well in advance, especially for weekend seatings. The chefs must obviously be doing something right or they wouldn't have so many people prepared to pay the fairly high prices and the relatively mature crowd have few complaints.

Mon-Sat 11.30-2.30, 5.30-10.30

Meal for two: £29 (Chicken in cream sauce)

Mediterranean

La Tasca

9 Weekday Cross (0115) 959 9456

Tapas is just about the ultimate party food. You don't like calamari? Cool. I'll have your

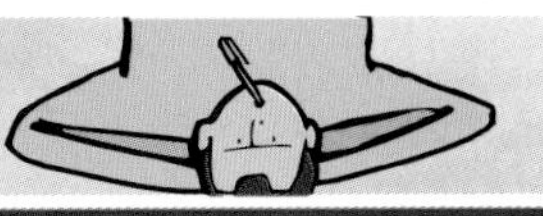

share, you can have my mushrooms. The best way to enjoy it is to get a table full of mates, oil liberally with plenty of sangria, and plough in. As well as decent Spanish food, the popularity of La Tasca also guarantees a lively atmosphere in the evenings when it gets very busy. Those just enjoying a bottle of cerveza spill out onto the outdoor patio during the summer months, when the restaurant's Weekday Cross location acts as a prime spot for watching the fashion conscious crowd descend upon the Lace Market for a night's bar surfing.

Mon-Sat 12-12 (food till 11), Sun 12-10.30
Meal for two: £26 (Paella)

Others

Benton's

36-38 Heathcote Street, Hockley (0115) 959 9800

Well-established bistro with an excellent reputation. However, it doesn't quite make it into Nottingham's restaurant premier league. At its best, it can compete with any of the top places in town but there's the odd occasion and the odd dish that slightly miss the mark. The food on the whole though, is a good standard, the décor simple but pleasant, and the place is always lively. Situated just on the corner where Heathcote Street meets Lower Parliament Street it's a popular destination for people visiting the new ice arena.

Mon-Sat 12-2.30, 6-10.30, Sun 6-10
Meal for two: £35.50 (2-course fixed meal)

Scruffy's

198 Derby Road (0115) 947 0471

The area around Derby Road and Canning Circus has a good reputation for restaurants and that's thanks largely to Scruffy's. It's been consistently popular for years thanks to its quality food and excellent value. This success can only be set to continue as this part of the city grows a residential hotspot. The basic and tasty food coupled with the friendly atmosphere attracts a mixed crowd of locals, students, and the occasional thesps from the playhouse.

Mon-Fri 6-11, Sat 12-11, Sun 6-10.30
Meal for two: £24 (Pork & leak bangers n mash)

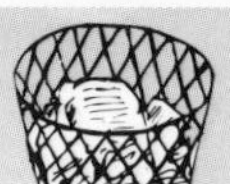

Scruffy's

47 Stoney Street (0115) 911 6333

This city centre sister restaurant to the Derby Road Scruffy's is equally popular and provides a similarly appealing menu. Being so close to nearly all the best bars in Nottingham it generates a more lively atmosphere as many of the customers are gearing up for a night out. It's also particularly popular for parties, and can cater for surprisingly large groups.

Mon-Fri 6-11, Sat 12-11, Sun 6-10.30
Meal for two: £29 (12oz Scruffy burger)

World Service

Newdigate House, Castlegate
(0115) 847 5587

Relative newcomer but firmly established as one of the most popular restaurants in town. Impressive and exclusive surroundings and a quality menu inspired by the four corners of the world have placed this in the top echelons of the city's restaurants.

Mon-Sat 12-2.30, 6.30-10.30,
Sun 12-3.30, 7-9pm
Meal for two: £35.90 (Pan-fried veal kidneys in puff pastry)

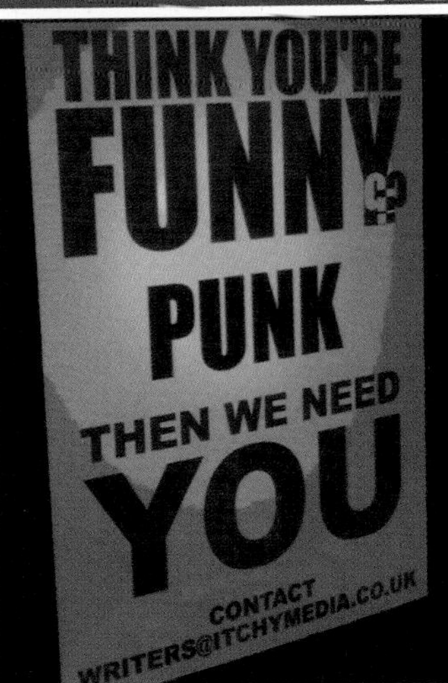

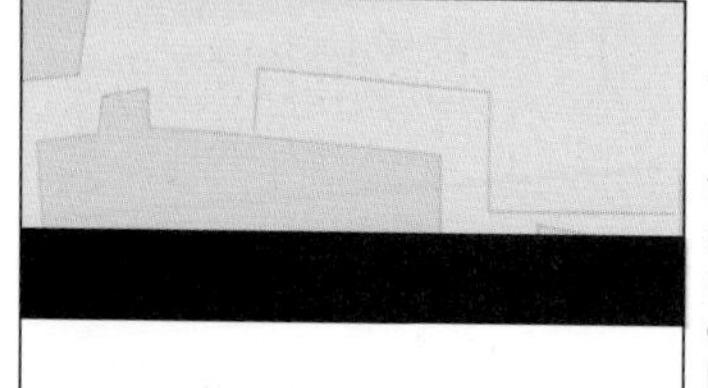

cafés

www.itchynottingham.co.uk

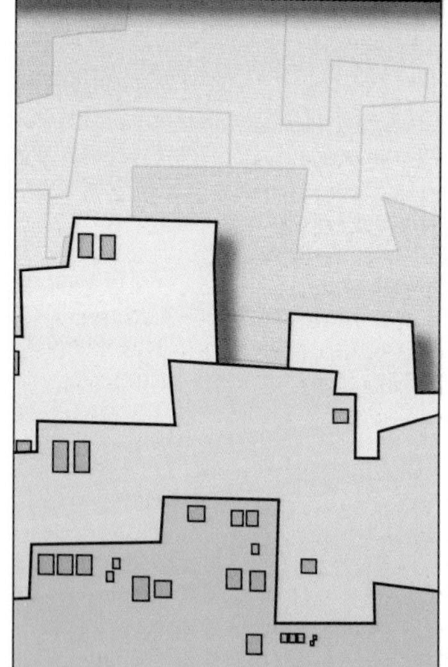

Café Nero

19 Bridlesmith Gate (0115) 950 0911

More of a modern style coffee shop than a traditional café. If you're out and about shopping round the trendy Bridlesmith area you might want to try and pick up a pair of Prada oven gloves if you're planning to get lunch here as the toasted sarnies seem to have an incredible capacity for heat retention.

Toasted ham panini £3.25 (be careful)
Mon-Fri 7-7, Sat 8am-7pm, Sun 10-5pm

Delifrance

3-5 Houndsgate (0115) 959 9045

French style boulangerie and café with adjoining sandwich shop. It's not particularly cheap to eat in, but they do good baguettes to takeaway at reduced prices. 'Formidablé'!

Brie and bacon baguette £4.05
Mon-Sat 8-5.30, Sun 10-4.30

Maid Marian Café

41 Friar Lane (0115) 952 8484

The old faithful Sherwood Forest/Robin Hood motif that local businesses are so reliant on is in full effect at this traditional English café. Don't expect a medieval banqueting hall though, this is your standard bacon butty and pot of tea greasy spoon, with a few shonky pictures of local legends adorning the walls.

Egg, chips, beans and tea £2.25
Mon-Sat 8am-6pm

Joel's Soho

8 Broad Street, Hockley

Stylish and relaxed café bar in the heart of the trendy Hockley area. Big breakfasts for those that want them, and also a selection of

interesting and bizarrely named sandwiches that are a cut above most café fare. May also be licensed to sell alcohol by the time you're reading this.
Flash fried salmon with lemon £5.25
Mon-Thu 9-9, Fri-Sat 9-2am

Parkers
89 Abbey Street, Dunkirk
(0115) 978 1569
Proper hangover-easing greasy spoon café and butty shop, this place is a genuine life-saver. It's also ideally located round the corner from the Queens Medical Centre in case any of the regulars require the occasional triple heart bypass.
Bacon bap £1.95
Mon-Sat 7am-6pm, Sun 9-4pm

Thompson Coffee Shop
20 Pelham Street (0115) 958 8443
Genuinely captures the authentic atmosphere of the continental style coffee shop, complete with that casual arrogance and dismissive superiority that French service industry workers have got off to a tee.
Sun-dried tomato and mozzarella £2.20
Mon-Sat 7am-5, Sun 10-3

Sandwich Shops

E@t me
Low Pavement (0115) 958 8089

Flavour of Hockley
2 Goosegate, Hockley, (0115) 950 7943

Hockley Sandwich Shop
8 Goosegate, Hockley (0115) 952 0366

Fresh
13 Goosegate, Hockley (0115) 924 3336

Internet Cafés

Alphanet
4 Queen Street (0115) 956 6988
Modern internet café and sandwich shop. Gaming and printer services also available.
Internet access £2 p/h before 12pm, £4 after. Regular offers and discounts for OAPs and students. Sandwiches £1.75
Mon-Wed and Sat 9.30am-8.30pm, Thu-Fri 9.30am-10.30pm

Vans
Broad Street (0115) 924 2409
Relaxed café offering Internet and printer services. Good selection of fresh juices too.
Internet access £3 p/h
All wraps and toasties £1.90
Mon-Sun 9am-11pm

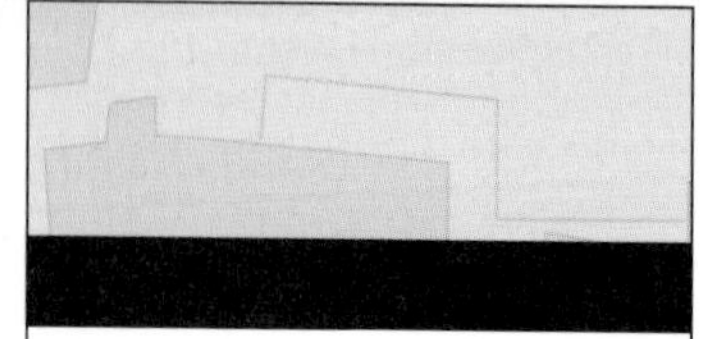

bars

www.itchynottingham.co.uk

Excess all Areas

One of the best things about Nottingham is the compact city centre, eliminating the loss of valuable drinking time when carting between boozers. However, despite the fact that you could probably cover most areas of the city centre on a night out, chances are you won't. The city breaks down into distinctive areas, and although there's inevitably a crossover it's worth having an idea of the different kinds of night out on offer:

The Canalside

The Canalside area, which is a stone's throw from the train station, was really kicked into life by the arrival of **Via Fossa** and **Bar Risa** a couple of years ago. Quickly followed by the **Waterfont** and then the **Canalhouse**, it has become something of a destination in its own right rather than just a calling point on your way into town. Truly the most mixed clientele of any of the areas mentioned here, it attracts students, happy hour chasers, the pre-Ocean crowd, the odd poser, and people moving on to other parts of town. If the sun starts shining for more than five minutes, the outside patio areas turn into a scene from Woodstock with half naked revellers covering every spare inch of lounging space. My

A MELLOW MIX OF SPIRIT AND SOUL.
THAT FLAVOURS WHATEVER IT TOUCHES.

FEEL THE
PRESENCE

TREVOR NELSON, DJ

Try it with soda and ice in a wild club.

advice is to take a Germanic approach to seat reservation and get your coat down on a prime spot sometime in April, return about 3 months later and arrogantly demand your place in the sun.

Hockley

Dissertations, pah. I'm off to study the culminate effects of vodka, Red Bull, and continental lager. A genuine mix of students, younger locals and the odd arty intellectual type all find something to float their boat in Hockley. The thick of the action can always be found in **Revolution**, but more laid back alternatives can be discovered down **Broad Street**. **Wax** can get pretty hectic at the weekends but regularly tempts the **Broadway** cappuccino crew from across the street when it hosts its mid-week **Culturel** and **Scientifique** nights. You can generally get away with trainers and denims at most places, but don't blame me if **Synergy** or the **Market Bar** get a bit shirty. Come five past eleven everyone heads up to the **Social**, as it's free in and it sells more booze.

Eleven

Brass Monkey

The Lace Market

You've had a hard day in front of your iMac and you deserve a gin and tonic. Your Ralph Lauren shirt or white stilettos aren't going to impress anyone in the **Glasshouse** so get that black Paul Smith number out of the wardrobe (whilst putting your trainers back in it.). Leave the Vauxhall Astra at home, but bring your Audi key ring if you want to impress the regulars in **Brass Monkey** or the **Sugar Bar**. If it's not past your bedtime when **Bluu Bar** shuts then on to the **Lizard Lounge**. Impress/piss off everyone in the queue by blagging your way in, but be warned, rejection can seriously damage your street cred, and is highly probable if you're wearing checks with stripes, brown with black or other similar fashion faux pas'.

Market Square

Time to get the suit off and the pulling gear on. And for a night round Market Square that means your best YSL shirt and shoes for you fellas, and your lowest-cut top and highest-cut skirts for you ladies. Bacardi Breezers all round as you make your way from **The**

Square to **Yates's** calling in at the **Goose** on the way. If you've had your fill of pumping dance cheese by 11pm, then it's kebab time, but if you've yet to pull, pull your finger out and head down to **Ocean**, **The Works** or the **The Palais**, or get a taxi to **Isis**.

Upper Parliament Street

I know, it's not really an area but it deserves a mention. I trust no UPS regulars will be looking at this anyway (reading a book? That's something that posh people do.)

All bars operate to normal licensing hours unless otherwise stated.

Bar Humbug

Friar Chambers, 26a Friar Lane
(0115) 8405160

It could be a case of 'what no carpet?' should the usual Market Square crowd wander in here by mistake, although that's unlikely as the understated entrance has none of the chrome, mirrors or neon lighting so attractive to muscle-bound meatheads and fake-tan tarts. Remarkably for such a central location Bar Humbug manages a courtyard for some summer drinking so you can easily forget where you are for an hour or two. The bar interior is bright and colourful enough to cheer up the most miserly soul and even the most Scrooge-like amongst you can't knock the value of the food.

Chicken Wrap £5.45
Happy Hour Mon, Thurs, Fri 5-8pm, Wed, Thurs, 5-10.30pm approximately 30% off cocktails

Bar None

Stoney Street, The Lace Market
(0115) 941 7072

There's been a late bar of some description in this spot for years. Formerly the Academy, it's now back, after a brief hiatus and a much needed bit of renovation, as Bar None. Whilst nothing drastic has happened to the interior, the spot of paint and polish has certainly done the trick, and it's again packed out with a lively crowd. Easily missed, apart from when the queues start building up, first time visitors are often surprised by this smart and popular cellar bar. Whilst only open Thursday/Friday/Saturday nights it retains the feel of a bar rather than a nightclub, thanks in part to the fact that the DJs don't

seem as intent on deafening the crowd like they do at most places. Bar None is also available for private hire through the week.
Thu-Sat 9pm-2am

Brass Monkey

11 High Pavement, The Lace Market
(0115) 840 4101

Had a reputation for a fairly strict door policy when it opened, but this seems to have relaxed slightly, now that a regular crowd has been established. Being one of the first bars of its type in the Lace Market, Brass Monkey's influence is certainly being felt in some of the newer Nottingham drinking

venues, with dark wooden panelling and rich luxurious tones replacing beechwood and cream as the design staple. The main criticism of Brass Monkey was that the narrow layout led to some heavy congestion when things got busy, with the main bar/seat/toilet routes suffering near total gridlock at times. Thankfully now the upstairs bar is open, and this should help considerably. Weather permitting Friday night is barbecue night, when you can enjoy some wicked food washed down with Pimms. How civilised.
Mon-Sat 12-12. Sun 12-10.30
Selection of bar snacks £1.90 each
Happy Hour Mon-Sun 5-8, Wed 5-11
Selected beers £1.75, large house wine £2.50, house spirits £1.50, cocktails from £1.80

Bar Risa

British Waterways Building, Canal Street
(0115) 958 9922

Smart modern bar in the landmark British Waterways building. With the canalside patio drinking area outside it's guaranteed to be busy when the weather's good, and excellent 2-4-1 drinks offers ensures popularity even if it gets a bit grim out there. The bar itself is spread over two floors, with upstairs forming a large mezzanine area looking over the main bar. There are a number of comfy settees, but you've got to be quick, especially during peak periods, to have a chance of getting one. Jongleurs comedy club upstairs may have some of the top names from the comedy circuit but you're unlikely to see anything funnier than someone walking, by mistake, up the spiral staircase which leads to nowhere and banging their swede on the ceiling (I've seen it happen). Whether you're on the way into town or making a night of it around the canal, Bar Risa is well worth calling in for one, or preferably two for one.

Steak and onion sandwich £3.75
Happy Hour Sun-Wed 5-8pm, Thu-Sat 4-7, 2 for 1 most drinks

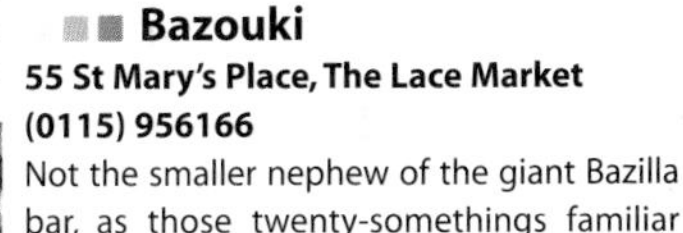

Bazouki

55 St Mary's Place, The Lace Market
(0115) 956166

Not the smaller nephew of the giant Bazilla bar, as those twenty-somethings familiar with Japanese cartoons from the late 70s might think, but quite literally the most colourful place in town. Handily placed (for me) for an after work pint, this multi-coloured Mediterranean style bar is particularly popular with folk who ply their respective trades in the offices and studios nearby.

Quite pleasant through the week, I can't comment on what it's like at the weekend, as I've been advised by my GP, to avoid wind tunnels, Primal Scream concerts, and anywhere else where the volume level exceeds 150 decibels.

Happy Hour 8-11pm Wed, doubles £2, pints £1.50

Berlins

1 Hockley (0115) 948 1899

Like a twisted vision of the future, from some cheap, direct to video, post apocalyptic, 80s action movie, Berlins is an acquired taste, albeit, in the same way that methylated spirits are. The fact that proudly displayed oxymoronic proclamations like 'All drinks £1 all day, before 6', can remain unchallenged, gives an indication to the mental capacity of most of the crowd. Lateral thinking may be beyond most of them, but they're quite inclined to have a stab at lateral drinking, as an inability to stand, shouldn't stand in the way of a true piss-cart's ability to consume cheap alco-pops.

Bluu

Stoney Street, the Lace Market (0115) 950 5359

Well blow me if it isn't like a scene from 'St Elmo's Fire' every time I come in here. I don't know why the curious phenomenon of mixed sex social groups only seems to congregate in this specific venue but I had to mention it. Getting back to the reviews, Bluu bar is another impressive edition to the burgeoning Lace Market scene that caters in part to the growing number of local residents. Managing a bit more warmth than many new bars, the style is modern without being clinical or sterile. Particularly welcoming is the large low-ceilinged basement area complete with the fattest sofas in town. The music policy is curious to say the least at times: I'm all for eclecticism, but drum 'n' bass and 10cc? In keeping with many nearby places there's a fairly strict door policy in operation from Thursdays to Saturdays (so, sorry I can't tell you what it's like then).

Open 11am-12am Mon-Wed. 11am-1am Thurs-Sat. 11am-10.30pm Sun

Grilled chicken with gruyere sandwich £4.95

The Broadway

14-18 Broad Street (0115) 952 1551

A real conundrum The Broadway; it's just a large, basically kitted-out room inside a cinema, with nothing particularly outstanding to speak about. So how come it's one of our favourite bars in town? To be honest I don't really know. Maybe it's the wealth of seats and reasonably priced drinks, or the way you get academic bookworms sitting around reading Proust and Nietzsche at one table, and idiots like us at the next. Maybe the fact it's one of the few places you can hold a conversation without screaming your lungs out. It's irrelevant why it works, it just does. It won't be to everyone's taste as it's much too chilled for some people, and anyone intent on showing off their new Prada jacket may be disappointed by the complete indifference with which they'll be met.

Food menu changes daily, most dishes £5-7

Canalhouse Bar

48-52 Canal Street (0115) 955 5011

Probably the most innovatively designed bar in the Canal Wharf area, and, to my knowledge, the only drinking establishment around with a canal running through it. The patio area outside is the only one along the canal that actually offers a bit of shade for the rare occasions it gets too hot, and the bar itself has excellent air conditioning, making it a prime spot for summer drinking. Inside there's wrought iron foot bridges and exposed brickwork giving the place plenty of character. As with all the bars along this part of town the clientele are a real mixed bag with students rubbing shoulders happily with locals. A major plus here is the bar food, which has to get a mention: top quality and fair prices.

Caesar salad with chicken and bacon strips £4.95

Student drinks offers on Tuesday and Wednesday nights

Casa

12-18 Friar Lane (0115) 979 9222

The longer standing of the city's two Casas, this large Friar Lane bar still gets our vote as one of the best places in town for a liquid lunch. The food is top-notch value, the place is cool and laidback, and the drinks menu is temptingly diverse. Even if I'm on an enforced period of alcohol abstinence I can't help nipping in to enjoy the chilled vibe over a cup or two of coffee (although those free Danish pastries with the itchy card are starting to take a toll on my waistline). Things of course liven up in the evenings, but even then it remains that bit more

relaxed than most. A sure fire test of a bars quality is how well it draws you in, and even on the biggest pub crawl, one pint just never seems enough in here.

Chicken with spinach and pesto £5.95
Happy Hour 5-7pm every night, 2 pint pitchers £6.50 (5-11pm Tue & Thu), Classic cocktails £2.95

Casa

The Arkwright Building, Trent Bridge
(0115) 985 2287

Having only opened in late 2000 this is a welcome addition to the Trent Bridge drinking options. Weather permitting, it's one of the prime spots in the city for outdoor drinking during the summer months. Trent Bridge may not be the most imposing structure, but the banks of the river, with the passing swans and rowing boats, are a particularly decent place to while away a few hours drinking the best pints of Stella in Nottingham. The main changes from the buildings previous incarnation as a pretty

average pub can be seen inside. Gone are the pool tables, fruit machines and TVs, and the whole place now has a fresh modern style. Obviously it's a calling point for people heading into town from West Bridgford, but there also seems to be plenty of people content to settle down and make a night of it.

Casa chicken special £7.95

Happy Hour 5-7pm every night, 2 pint pitchers £6.50 Classic cocktails £2.95

Edwards

Upper Parliament Street (0115) 941 2609

Erm, ah, ho hum, ho hum, mmmm, erm, mmm, I'm struggling a bit here. Quite possibly the least remarkable bar in town. Oh well here goes. It's big (ish), and there's lots of wood and stuff, and they do a few drink offers, and is anybody still reading this? Just move on.

Eleven

23 Goosegate, Hockley (0115) 859 8831

Like Brass Monkey with a sunroof, the enigmatically named Eleven throws a bit of Lace Market style into the Hockley mixer. With dark wooden panelling and plush seating it's pretty much unrecognisable from its previous incarnation as a Greek restaurant, and thankfully, along with the panoramic view of the Greek countryside that covered the entire far wall, the underage drinkers have been moved on and replaced by a slightly wiser and better looking crowd. A newcomer to the scene, early signs are quite promising and it has a definite cool vibe.

Chicken satay £6.25

Escape

5-7 Castle Road (0115) 947 3355

It seems blindingly obvious now, but why didn't anyone think of it sooner? The area directly around Nottingham Castle is one of the nicest parts of town, but for years it's only been lightly populated by a couple of unremarkable drinking venues (excluding 'The Trip', which is a bit further down anyway). Considering the proximity to the private Park Estate, and that the adjacent Ropewalk area is the main centre for Nottingham's legal businesses, then you can appreciate that this part of town is swimming with cash. Partly with this in mind, I'm sure, Escape was opened to bring the kind of modern stylish minimalism more commonly associated with the new Lace Market bars. Being on the side of such a steep hill, the bar is split levelled to accommodate the slope, and this helps to lend a little interest to the layout. Cleverly, and a little optimistically, the front windows have been designed to completely open up when the sun's shining, and provide one of the best spots in town for outdoor drinking.

Thai spiced chicken fritters £9.50

The Establishment

3 Broadway, The Lace Market
(0115) 911 1060

Whatever happened to Franz Carr eh? He used to be in here an hour after final whistle every Saturday (even when he was supposed to be playing in Serie B)*. Goes to show how quickly things change in the fickle world of bar culture. This place was the 'dogs' when it opened a few years back. Impressive in style and scale, it really put the Lace Market on the map for socialising. Beach flooring and chrome banisters may no longer be the height of cool, but the fact that it now seems pretty ordinary is more a reflection on the developments in the immediate vicinity. It's still OK but rapidly approaching the end of its shelf life. Revamp please.

** this may not actually be true, and itchy Ltd would like to stress that in no way should it be inferred that Franz Carr has been anything less than a model professional throughout his career. Wherever the hell he is now.*

Happy Hour 7-9 Fri & Sat. £1.50 selected pints plus other offers

Fashion

Middle Pavement (0115) 950 5850

As anyone who knows us will testify, fashion is something we at team itchy know little about. As this absence of sartorial elegance means we're generally denied entrance to exclusive classy places like this I've had to fall back on the old 'nose to window' school of journalism. I can see men in suits drinking cocktails with pretty ladies. Grand mahogany furniture and glamorous pictures of beautiful people. It all looks so good. Actually the smart dress policy is only really enforced at the weekend and the rest of the time it's accessible to plebs like us. As an up-market cocktail bar and restaurant, situated in the heart of Nottingham's shopping area, this is the ideal place to call if you've been hammering the plastic down Bridlesmith Gate, especially in summer when you can chill at one of the outdoor tables.

Mon-Thu 10am-11pm, Fri-Sat 10am-2am, Sun 12-10.30

Thai green curry £8.95

The Glasshouse

High Pavement, The Lace Market (0115) 950 6888

Despite the impressive size Glasshouse manages a sense of intimacy, and enough quirky design features to distinguish it from the crowd. The leather padded booths may be evocative of the bouncy-castles of your youth, but 'It's a Knockout' style antics aren't to be encouraged after too many vodka Red Bulls. Considering its location, there's a relatively relaxed door policy in operation, (even I've never been refused) but one downside in my opinion is the rather unforgiving lighting; you might revel in the bleached white brilliance if you're one of the beautiful people, but the rest of you can join me in the somewhat dimmer downstairs bar.

Mon-Sat 11am-12am, Sun 12-10.30

Rissotto of wild mushrooms & parmesan £8

Katmandu

The Old Bus Depot, Mansfield Road, Sherwood (0115) 911 1910

Legend has it that this is a golden temple full of wonders in a mystical far away land. OK so it's a former bus depot in Sherwood, but it is full of the wonders of bar-land. It's also temple-like in its proportions with an extremely high ceiling and a huge balcony area. The opening of Katmandu in 2000 was a reflection of Sherwood's status as an up and coming area. In complete contrast to the nearby pubs, this is an extremely modern and cool bar kitted-out in bright summery colours that manages to avoid feeling cold or empty despite the impressive size. Considering it's the first bar of its type in this part of town it's particularly brave being so bloody big.

Beef Bourgignon £5.25

The Loft

217 Mansfield Road (0115) 924 0213

Only a short while ago you wouldn't have found anything remotely resembling a cool independent bar anywhere outside Hockley, but it's a reflection of the change in drinking culture that places like The Loft can now survive outside the city centre. For years Mansfield Road has been a haven of traditional boozers and budget restaurants but there's now a genuine alternative for the locals and Mapperley Park residents. It's also a popular calling point for people heading into town from Sherwood and the north side of the city. It's a fairly small venue but the designers have been economical with the space and consequently the front doors open up almost directly into the toilets, so throw an immediate left up the stairs to the bar area itself which is light and airy. The lack of direct competition in the vicinity also means that the Loft attracts a regular crowd of familiar faces including many 'musos' from the nearby recording studios.

Lloyds

Carlton Street (0115) 9881660

In its day Lloyds was one of the classiest places in town, but it's a sign of the times that it now stands as Hockley's own little piece of Market Square. After a period of dwindling popularity, Wetherspoons took over and the prices came down marginally faster than the tone.

Chicken Wraps £3.49 (including free drink)

Liberty's

Upper Parliament Street (0115) 988 1491

Another typically classy Upper Parliament Street bar that's always packed-out with dubious looking moustached men (and

Sebor
nunc est
bibendum
CZECH REPUBLIC
ABSINTH
50 cl
55% vol

Sebor

women) getting liberated from their dole cheques and their senses. The décor is best described as an 80s style interpretation of Americana, or in other words crap with chrome on. With so many disturbing sights on show you'll be relieved that the lighting is mercifully dim. This also diminishes the chances of catching the eye of a tattooed bruiser who'll accuse you of eyeing up his bird/mam/pint, and kill you. Of course if you're an Upper Parliament Street regular then you'll feel immediately at home, all others would be advised to make a break for freedom at the first opportunity.

Number 10

67 Upper Parliament Street
(0115) 9475842

Considering its address, the name Number 10 evidently presumes a level of innumeracy amongst its clientele. As well as any deficiency with figures, one look at an average punter would also suggest a complete lack of social graces, basic communication skills, anything remotely resembling a sense of style, and in many cases teeth.

Pitcher and Piano

High Pavement, The Lace Market
(0115) 958 6081

Despite the complete overhaul of Nottingham's bar culture in the last three or four years, the Pitcher and Piano is yet to be surpassed as the most visually impressive drinking establishment in town. As a church conversion you won't be surprised to hear that it's striking in scale with the original spire

forming a focal point. A very cool place for daytime drinking as the size dictates that you can always get a table and chill out, and even when things get a bit livelier in the evenings the music remains at a dignified level.

Thai green curry chicken £6

Red Back Bar

Upper Parliament Street (0015) 953 1531

Roll-up, roll-up. See the bearded lady. Run in terror from the tattooed giant. Laugh at the spotty boy racer. Yes it's another freak show in the circus of Upper Parliament Street. After a tough week of sitting on your mam's settee and watching soap operas what could be better than blowing your hard earned dole money on copious quantities of piss cheap lager? Well almost anything in my opinion, but what do I know? Just as in the animal kingdom, there's a definite hierarchy in operation amongst the regulars here. I haven't quite cracked the code by which this pecking order is established, but I believe it somehow incorporates factors such as quality of facial hair, proximity of tattoos to facial region, depth of step in wedge haircut, number of sovereign rings, and of course size of spoiler taped onto your dad's Vauxhall Nova.

Revolution

7 Broad Street, Hockley (0115) 947 4578

Crowd participation sees the Russian theme taken to its logical conclusion on Saturday nights here, when the throngs of would-be revellers form an orderly line that stretches half way down Broad Street in the style of an Eastern Block bread queue. Livelier and louder than the likes of Broadway across the street, it's generally full of young lads and lasses throwing the fire water down their necks in preparation for a night on the tiles. The theme in these chain bars may be far from revolutionary (pun intended) but the room could well be spinning after one too many hot chilli vodkas, although downing enough 70% vodka certainly helps with the spirit of glasnost.

Club sandwich £3.75

Scruffys

198 Derby Road (0115) 947 0471

Well renowned as a restaurant, those kind people at Scruffy's have recently extended the premises to incorporate a seperate bar area. It's only small but it's a cool little space and is presently the only real drinking alternative to the traditional pubs. Just by the entrance to the Park estate and near many new residential developments this bar is sure to prove a popular haunt in this rapidly up-and-coming area.

Sinatra's

16 Chapel Bar (0115) 941 1050

A modern day 'Sands Casino' where fast living and faster women meet head on. Tough talking and hard drinking go hand in hand, and hell-raising is the norm. Um, no, actually 'Rat Pack' style behaviour will be very much frowned upon in this rather sedate bar and restaurant, whose clientele is made up primarily of dining couples and pre-theatre cocktail sippers. The name comes from the pictures of Old Blue Eyes, and the countless other stars of stage and screen that cover every spare inch of wall in this upmarket and highly civilised establishment. Late licence at the weekends, but don't expect it to be filled with clubbers gearing up for a big night on the dancefloor, it's strictly professional types. Zooby dooby doo.

Bar remains open until 12am Fri-Sat
No entry after 11pm
Bacon and Brie sandwich £5.25

Slug and Fiddle

Upper Parliament Street (0115) 924 1779

It was a brave and pioneering experiment that was always going to carry high risks. No-one had previously attempted to put any class into an Upper Parliament Street bar. Predictably the style transplant was rejected by its host, and it all seems like a bit of a waste of effort. Most UPS regulars wouldn't know the difference between a leather Chesterfield and a deckchair anyway, and rosewood flooring has an unfortunate habit of not hiding spilled cider and alco-pops quite as well as gaudily striped carpet tiles. Nice try though.

Slug and Lettuce

12 Low Pavement (0115) 958 9100

For some time now the Slug has been waging war with the adjacent Caffé Uno via the medium of the chalk-board. Proceedings have gotten quite bitchy, with sly wisecracks being parried by snooty counter jibe. With awesome punnery of the standard of 'lettuce entertain you' somebody has clearly missed their calling as a writer of city guides. Evidently heeding my words in itchy Nottingham 2001, the monolithic front doors have been replaced by an entrance that would no longer stop Popeye in his tracks on a kingsize spinach-rush. This change of 'door policy' may well see an influx of the frail and elderly, aware that they've been missing out all this time on the comfy ambience and very decent food. However, should Gran make it in any time after about 6pm she's unlikely to be impressed by the music, the crapness of which is equalled only by the inadequacy of the system on which it's played.

Smoked chicken ciabatta with parsnip chips and hot gooseberry chutney £4.95

The Social

23 Pelham Street (0115) 950 5078

One of Nottingham's best bars, The Social was the first place of real significance to have a late licence when it opened in '99. That fact alone insured its initial popularity, but as the number of late bars thankfully grows The Social has maintained its standing as a favourite with the young dudes and dudessess thanks to its relaxed door policy and cool crowd. The crowded nature of the seating and reasonable level of the jukebox makes downstairs very much the place for social interaction/talking bollocks to complete strangers. Things upstairs are more focused on the dancefloor, and although the predominantly funk and soul-led soundtrack is hardly innovative, it certainly has broad appeal. Also a great compact venue for live gigs, where you'll often find the next

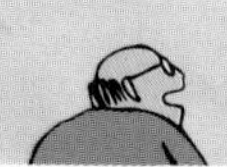

big things (Coldplay, Starsailor) playing, or returning favourites (the Stereo MCs will go down as a classic).

Mon-Thu 11am-12am, Fri-Sat 11am-2am, Sun 12-10.30pm
Selection of sandwiches £2.50, main meals £4.50
Happy hour 5-9 Mon-Fri. Pint of Becks £1.50, house spirits £1.50

South Bank Bar

Trent Bridge, West Bridgford
(0115) 945 5541

It's something of a national institution to sit in the pub with a pint or three and watch the big Premiership match on Sunday, or Monday, or Champions League on Tuesday/Wednesday or Nationwide on Thursday and Friday. I don't know, they'll be playing matches on Saturdays next. Arguably the best place to watch the footy in all Nottingham, and certainly the best south of the river.

Chicken tikka and Cajun chicken duo £6.25
Happy hour 5-8pm. House wine £5
10-11pm selected doubles £2.75

Sugar Bar

Broadway, The Lace Market
(0115) 947 5083

Popular 2-floored bar that recently improved itself with a late licence. As exclu-

DON'T GET INTIMIDATED BY THEIR EYE CONTACT

sive as its Lace Market neighbours, it's packed at the weekend with a smart young crowd intent on enjoying themselves and spending their hard earned. Wednesday nights now feature live music, with different salsa bands playing every week for you to shake your thang to. As well as being a good place to call in on your rounds, Sugar Bar is also a top venue for private parties where you'll be offered some quality drinks discounts like double vodka Red Bull for 2 quid. Can't say fairer than that, can you?

Steak and onion baguette £6.25
Happy hour 5-8.30 everyday. Offers on selected bottles and spirits

Synergy

9 Broad Street, Hockley (0115) 924 1555

Synergy: The union of two separate elements that come together in perfect harmony to create something stronger than the sum of its parts. Whatever. Synergy pitches itself as the most exclusive bar in Hockley, bringing hitherto unseen levels of door scrutiny to Broad Street. Whether you see this as a good or bad thing will depend on the cut of your cloth. Those 'lucky' enough to get in on a Saturday night will be rewarded with one of the best selections of drinks in town, where you can check for yourself the synergy when Bullet bourbon meets Coca-Cola.

Chicken and duck stir fry £6.95
Happy hour 5-7pm. 2 for 1 cocktails

That Café Bar

43 Broad Street, Hockley (0115) 952 6116

Something of a hidden gem, That Café Bar doesn't really attract the throngs from along the street, and it doesn't try to either. Small and intimate it serves excellent food and is usually busy with diners throughout the week, but at the weekend it definitely takes on the role of bar rather than café as it gets nicely filled with a knowing crowd.

Cajun black bean salmon £4.95

Voodoo Bar

Goosegate, Hockley (0115) 950 1003

Theme bars can be a bit over the top banging the message home can't they? Yes, you might be an Arctic-style Eskimo cocktail shack, but shut the window please, it's freezing. Thankfully the black magic motif in here is limited to a couple of voodoo-inspired wall paintings, so virgin blood cocktails and sacrificial goat heart sandwiches are relievingly omitted from the menu.

Mardi Gras paninni £3

"OI, WHAT ARE YOU LOT STARING AT!?"

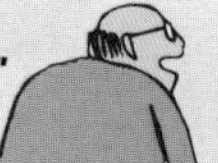

Walkabout

Friar lane (0115) 941 0990

Sadly not a shrine to a young Jenny Agutter, but rather a bar dedicated to Aussie culture (that'll be drinking then). Big, brash and lacking in sophistication, are just a few accusations often levelled at our Antipodean cousins, and Walkabout does little to challenge the stereotypes, but what do you expect from a theme bar? There's a huge screen to watch the match on, but even with the plethora of channels available you'll probably struggle to find a sport that we can actually beat the Aussies at (they're even looking quite handy at proper football these days. Bastards).

Kangaroo steak £4.50

The Waterfront

Canal Wharf, Canal Street (0115) 979 9111

It could have been somewhere: it could have been a contender. Possibly the least remarkable of the canal area bars this is a fairly standard place with less imagination than it's neighbours. Actually, being unremarkable hasn't hurt trade at all and the excellent location and regular drinks promotions have guaranteed a brisk trade. The Waterfront is a large two-floored bar with a sizeable outside seating area, and as with its neighbours, it's always packed out if the sun's shining, when the upstairs balcony acts as the crow's nest for some serious talent spotting

Chicken & black bean stir fry with rice £4.95

top 5 for... happy hours

1. Bar Risa
2. Casa
3. The Social
4. Brass Monkey
5. Bar Humbug

Wax

27 Broad Street (0115) 959 007

'I drink therefore I am'. Go to any Upper Parliament Street boozer and you're likely to have little problem finding a bar-room philosopher willing to enlighten you with their theories on the meaning of life. However, Wax would like to think the debate in here is stimulated more by the thirst for knowledge than the thirst for house doubles. With the Cultural and Scientifique nights that Wax has hosted for a number of years now it has cultivated something of a loyal following amongst arty and intellectual types. Broad minds may be welcome, but too many broad people could be problematic as the bar itself is rather narrow, and moving about can be very tricky when things get busy. If you manage to get a table and chair then get the beers in and you'll soon be talking nonsense and trying to sort out the worlds problems whilst either amusing to a point of pain or completely pissing off the couple of love birds trying to have a 'quiet drink' next to you.

Sirloin steak sandwich with fries £4.95

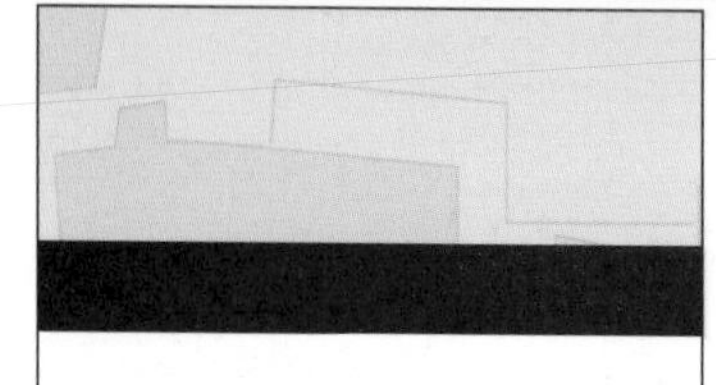

All pubs operate within normal licensing hours unless otherwise stated.

Bentinck Hotel

Station Street (0115) 958 0285

For those visiting Nottingham by rail, the Bentinck will almost certainly be the first public house you're faced with. Whether you should choose it as the place to introduce yourself to the city's drinking establishments is less certain. A small and traditional city centre pub, its proximity to the train and bus stations leads to a fairly transitory customer base and it isn't particularly welcoming, especially on match days (visitors from along the A52 would be particularly well advised to give it a wide berth) when it's packed with dodgy looking, tattoo covered Forest fans. Of course if you *are* a dodgy looking, tattoo covered Forest fan, I'll see you in there.

Byron's

North Church Street (0115) 947 2792

A large no nonsense pub, Byron's is a good place to watch the football and sink a few. The best thing is that it never seems to get ridiculously busy leading you to spend most of the match either trying to get a pint in or jostle for a decent view. With plenty of offers on all types of drinks, you can't go wrong here if you're a bit short of cash, (but watch out, as the combination of cheap drinks and a city centre location always lead to the occasional schizo coming in and trying intently to make you his new best friend). Whilst a perfectly fine place for the odd pint, we'd recommend giving the food a miss as it's pretty poor.

Food served Mon-Sat 12-5, Sun 12-4

Callaghan's

St James Street 0870 400 9062

Callaghan's Irish pub is a public bar that forms part of the Forte Posthouse Hotel. The Irish theme is thankfully understated and the place just has the feel of a traditional boozer. Thanks to the hideous Maid Marion Way that divides this side of town from the city centre you won't find many people calling in here on a night round Market Square, but if you're out and about around the Castle area then it's a decent place for a pint of the black stuff, especially as you can sup away until 1am.

Open 11am-1am

The Cremorne

Queens Walk, The Meadows (0115) 953 1199

Superficially this may appear to be a run of the mill, quiet local's pub, and a lot of the time it is. However if you're just popping in for a Sunday afternoon pint you may need to brace yourself. Firstly the giant projector screen comes down to show the footy, then the jukebox kicks in, followed by the world's loudest fruit machine, and just when you think you're reaching full sensory overload the fun really begins as the karaoke starts up.

The Dog and Topper

Sherwin Road, Lenton (0115) 941 9353

Off Studentville/Lenton this quirkily constructed modern pub has all the attributes to ensure its popularity amongst scholastic scroungers. Pool tables, satellite TV and solid value drinks and food promotions, what more could you ask for? The beer 'garden' at

the rear may not be the most picturesque but the main bar is a surprisingly pleasant place to watch busy people scurrying about outside doing trivial things, like, you know, going to work.

Food served 12-6pm

Fellows Morton & Clayton

54 Canal Street (0115) 950 6795

Alright geezer. Gimme some of them Bacardi Breezers and ten vodka Red Bulls. Wahey. I'm sorry, I think you want to be next door. All the action might be happening at those fancy new bars that have emerged around the canal area but this pub is not the place for bare-chested drinking games and alco-pop induced high jinks, so get a pint in and pipe down. The Fellows Clayton and Morton, sorry The Claymore Fentons...The Mellows Felton and..., no that's still not right is it. Tip 2, never call this pub by its full name; any abbreviations or variations of the above will suffice, as no one really knows what it's called.

Food served Mon-Sat 12-10pm, Sun 12-6pm

The Hogshead
11 Victoria Street (0115) 958 4825

Although only open for two or three years, The Hogshead has just had a renovation. Considering its appearance prior to this spit and polish, you wouldn't have put it at the top of the list of Nottingham pubs in need of regeneration, as it looked perfectly alright. However, this rare move of shutting the stable door prior to the horse bolting is to be commended, and other places could learn to keep on top of the game rather than waiting to fall into complete disrepair before even thinking about getting the paintbrush out. It's not a radical change, and they haven't gone crazy, they've just kept it looking a lot fresher than the majority of chain pubs. The Hogshead consequently strikes a nice balance; it doesn't profess to be a trendy independent Hockley bar, but nor is it a Market Square corporate cheese-fest.

Food served 12-7pm

The Grove
Abbey Bridge Roundabout
(0115) 941 06367

In contrast to the Dog and Topper that stands at the other side of Abbey Bridge Roundabout, the impressive looking Grove is a much more traditional boozer. Of course its location means you still get plenty of students in, it's just that they tend to be students of real ale and the art of dominos, rather than the all singing all dancing type.

The Limelight
Nottingham Playhouse, Wellington Circus (0115) 941 8467

Pleasant pub that attracts plenty of pre-theatre goers, and those looking for a bit more peace and quiet than that offered at most centrally located pubs. Forming part of the Nottingham Playhouse building you'll regularly see the odd thesp nipping in for a glass of Pimms, but don't assume anybody there wearing shades is a visiting Hollywood superstar; they're more likely just shielding their eyes from the potential death ray produced by the Sky Mirror sculpture.

Food served 12-8pm Mon-Sat, 12-2.30 Sun

The Lord Nelson

11 Thurgarton Street, Sneinton (0115) 911 0069

With its tidy little beer garden, this traditional pub is something of a haven amongst the terraced streets of Sneinton. For me it's definitely the nicest pub in this part of town and it certainly attracts a better class of punter than most Sneinton boozers, which are usually full of trampy dole-ites sucking cider through their toothless mushes.

Food served 12-2.30 Sunday only

Old Angel

7 Stoney Street, The Lace Market (0115) 950 2303

Despite all the development in the area and all the poncy new bars that are popping up on a daily basis, this Lace Market venue has stood staunchly to its guns as a slightly battered and crusty old pub. Consistently popular with the dreadlock and dungarees crew it also drags many in to sample its award winning vegetarian food.

Food served Mon-Sun 12-7pm

The Park

23 Arboretum Street (0115) 978 5914

Right, let's settle the confusion. The Arboretum is a park. The Park, which also used to be called The Arboretum, is the pub within said park. I hope that's cleared things up for you all. The pub, as we shall refer to it henceforth, is a popular student venue that's looking quite smart these days after its recent tarting up, and with the huge beer garden overlooking the rolling greens of the Arboretum it's an excellent place for al fresco alcohol consumption. Something of an irony then, that being a student pub, the best time to enjoy its location are through the summer months when the majority of its regulars are back in Kent annoying their mum and dad.

Food menu served 12-6pm. Jacket potatoes available after 6pm
Late licence until 12.30am Wed-Sat

The Roebuck

St James Street (0115) 979 3400

In a similar way that dog-years count sevenfold, when you factor in prices like £1.29 for a bottle of Stella, time spent in Wetherspoons must count as nearly double regular pub hours. Deceptively large with impressively high ceilings, slate flooring by the bar, and an interesting layout, The Roebuck is usually busy with a mixed clientele of the after-work crowd, students, the young and old. The drinks prices are as generous as expected, but you might be surprised by the absence of drunken old men or professional dole-ites. The other notable feature in all Wetherspoons pubs is the complete absence of music. Whilst initially somewhat alien, the ability to talk with your friends without resorting to screaming your lungs out is a blessed relief. The downside of being able to hear yourself speak is that everyone else can as well, and there's always one group who spoil things by doing their best Brian Blessed impressions. Unfortunately it's usually us.

Food served Mon-Sat 11-10, Sun 11-9.30

The Salutation

Maid Marion Way (0115) 988 1948

Although a Hogshead pub, the 'Sal' has bags of character and history. Its existence dates back to the time of the Civil War and it's another pub that lays claim to being the oldest in the city. Whilst the front of the pub is very picturesque, unfortunately the rear is blighted by the eyesore that is Maid Marion Way, but don't let that put you off as this is one of the better pubs in town.

Food served 12-7.30

The Trent Bridge Inn

2 Radcliffe Road, West Bridgford
(0115) 982 2786

One of the best-known pubs in Nottingham, the TBI is surprisingly unremarkable other than for its positioning. Forming one corner of the cricket ground and facing over Trent Bridge itself, it's something of a landmark location, but other than that it's a pretty standard pub. Pretty cavernous inside, but it certainly needs all its space on match days (cricket and football) when it gets rammed with either England fans drowning their sorrows after a trouncing from the Aussies, or Forest fans in similar need of comfort after another dismal draw with the likes of Crewe Alexander or Stockport County.

Turf Tavern

Upper Parliament Street (0115) 911 1719

Self proclaimed as the 'Friendliest pub in town'. Good job really considering that as this is one of the smallest pubs in town, there'd be nowhere to hide if it did all kick-off. Along with Langtry's next door, the Turf Tavern is a traditional contrast to the nearby Cornerhouse development. It also doesn't appeal to the mob from further along Upper Parliament Street, having instead a crowd whose missing teeth are a product of the ageing process rather than any propensity for violence.

Vat and Fiddle

Queens Bridge Road (0115) 985 0611

Humorously renamed after the opening of the close-by Inland Revenue office, the Vat and Fiddle (get it?) is probably the most welcoming of the pubs around the train station. Its most distinguishing feature is the on-site Castle Rock brewery ensuring that there's no excuse for the quality of the beer. However, the smell of fermenting hops and barley is a subject that divides opinion more than the Forest or County debate, and will therefore either greatly enhance your drinking experience or thoroughly nauseate you depending on your stance.

Food served 12-3pm

Via Fossa

44 Canal Street (0115) 947 3904

The first of the new developments in the canal wharf area, Via Fossa is an imposingly large pub with numerous bars and seating areas. It has a touch of gothic splendour coupled with a few quirky features and plenty of nooks and crannies to get lost in. During the week it vies for custom with the healthy competition from the nearby bars.

Food served Mon-Sat 12-10.30, Sun 12-10

Wetherspoons

Market Square (0115) 947 5034

I'm sure if I put my mind to it I could come up with something disparaging and cynical about this place. But what's the point. It is what it is, and if you want cheap booze and cheap food, and you don't mind putting up with a few cheap people, then welcome to Wetherspoons. Whilst these pubs never vary wildly, I would say that I actually prefer the Roebuck on St James Street, but as the saying goes 'you pays your (small amount of) money, you takes your choice'

Food served Mon-Sat 11-10, Sun 11-9.30

top 5 for...
outdoor drinking

1. Canal Wharf area
2. Casa (Trent Bridge)
3. Escape
4. The Park
5. Fashion

Yates's Wine Lodge

49 Long Row (0115) 947 3334

The classic calling point on any city centre piss crawl, you always know what you get with a Yates's. And that's loud music, loud people, and even louder shirts.

Food served Mon-Thu 12-8pm, Fri 12-6, Sat 12-3.30, Sun 12-5 approx times

Ye Olde Trip to Jerusalem

Brew House Yard (0115) 947 3171

One of several pubs that lays claim to the hotly disputed title of the oldest inn in England. The Trip has more character and history than most pubs in Nottingham put together. Being partially carved from the foot of the solid limestone cliff upon which sits Nottingham Castle it clearly dates back from a time when people were either a lot shorter or used to wear their Roundhead helmets to the pub, as some parts of the ceiling are dangerously low.

Food served 12-6pm

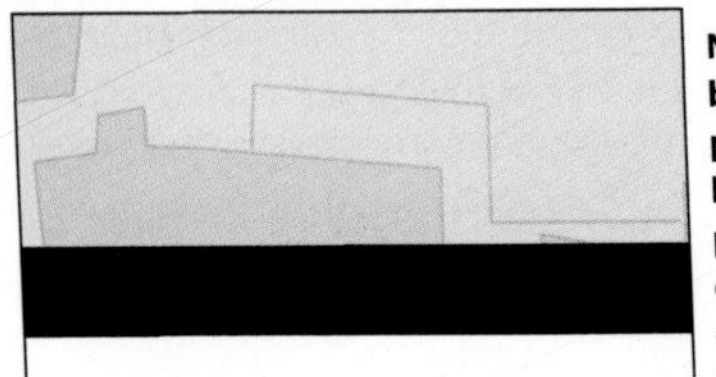

gay

www.itchynottingham.co.uk

in association with gay.uk.net

Nottingham is the exact gravitational belly button of the British Isles, so it's a popular place for people who are travelling across the county, to pop in and sample the beers/queers. The "Sheriff" boasts on the website: "Hardly anyone would even take a second glance at gay men holding hands in the street, or lesbians kissing in a supermarket!". Which is not necessarily a good thing, but then, we're bitter and twisted. Think yourselves lucky – maybe you'll have an encounter with the Sheriff of Nottingham.

Bars

@D2

74 Lower Parliament Street
(0115) 9502727

Formerly the typically old-fashioned gay pub the Admiral Duncan this venue got dragged into the 21st century (kicking and screaming no doubt) after the opening of NG1 next door. Wheelchair access.

Mon/Tue 8pm-late, Wed-Sat 8pm-2am, Sun 9pm-late

Jacey's

Heathcote Street, Hockley

Nottingham's newest gay bar. Increasingly more of a club than pub, the venue has a large dancefloor and regular dance music. No late license though. Fridays are regular male stripper nights, so watch the silk shirt with all that flying baby lotion.

Pub hours

Eternity @ Bugmans Bar

Willow Road, Lenton (0115) 950 2727

Exclusive for women with women in mind.

One of the Midland`s best female DJs is resident DJ Sesh. Features other monthly guest DJs, live bands and stand up comedians.
Last Saturday of month – 7.30pm till late

Pubs

Forresters Arms

St Anns Street (0115) 958 0432

Monday: Disco Night. Tuesday: Karaoke Night. Wednesday: Background Music Night. Thursday: Disco Night. Friday: Disco Night. Saturday: Disco Night. Sunday: Disco Night. Basically, this gaffe is a lezzy-run mixed gay pub with a disco area. OK? Sorted.
Pub hours

Forresters Inn

183 Huntingdon Street (0115) 941 9679

Popular mixed gay-friendly pub. Now under new (gay male) management, so check out www.itchynottingham.co.uk for details. Food is now being served from 12pm-7pm each day, offering basic but good quality meals for under £3. Mixed lesbian and gay crowd. Wheelchair access.
Pub hours

Clubs

NG1

76-80 Lower Parliament Street (0115) 958 8440

Nottingham's very own gay super club NG1 changed the Nottingham scene forever and revitalised the area around it. This 750 capacity club boasts 2 dancefloors, 3 bars and a café. OK, so what goes on? Check out www.itchynottingham.co.uk for reviews of the latest nights, but in the meantime, here's a brief run-down:

Wednesday: Commercial dance £2/£3
Thursday: Gay-friendly students free b4 11, £1 after
Friday: Funky tunes/handbag £4/£5
Saturday: Bounce/hard house/commercial dance £5/£6
Sunday: Stage bar show £1/£2. Mixed lesbian and gay crowd
Weds/Thu 10pm-2am, Fri/Sat 10pm-late, Sun 9pm-12am

The Mill

Woolpack Lane (0115) 964 4941

A mixed lesbian and gay crowd hang out in this stylish bar/club. There are two floors; upstairs dancefloor and DJ, downstairs pool (not swimming) and lifesize Jenga and Connect 4. Drinks promos most nights.
Mondays: Relax, 80s Revival Night
Tuesdays: Popmania
Wednesdays: Voltage
Sundays: Top Ten, 2-for-1 drinks.
11.30am-midnight throughout week

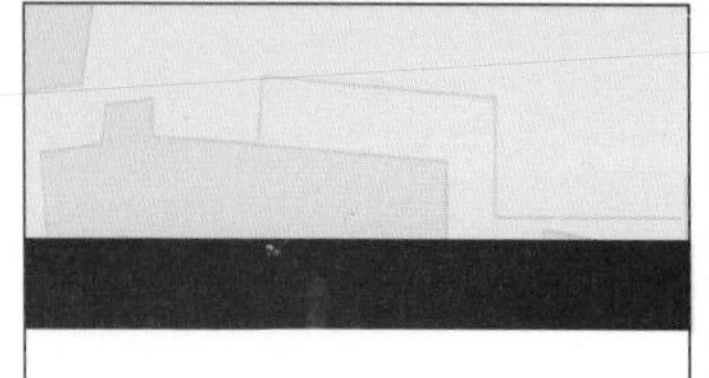

clubs

www.itchynottingham.co.uk

The Ballroom

Lenton Boulevard (0115) 942 0297

One of the biggest venues in Nottingham, The Ballroom is used by independent promoters for one-off and regular events. Obviously the kind of night varies depending on the events, which can be anything from hip-hop or techno to drum 'n' bass all-nighters. Formerly the Marcus Garvy centre, the place has had something of a reputation over the years for attracting a dodgy element, but whilst there's usually a number of hooded and huddled shady-looking characters around the periphery, the actual numbers of unsavoury incidents are probably negligible.

Bar None

Stoney Street, The Lace Market (0115) 941 7072

Traverses the hinterland between bar and club and pretty much manages to provide the best of both worlds. There's DJs and dancefloor action but it doesn't totally dominate proceedings, and there's plenty of opportunity to drink all night and talk bar nonsense without being deafened or danced on by pogo-ing lunatics.

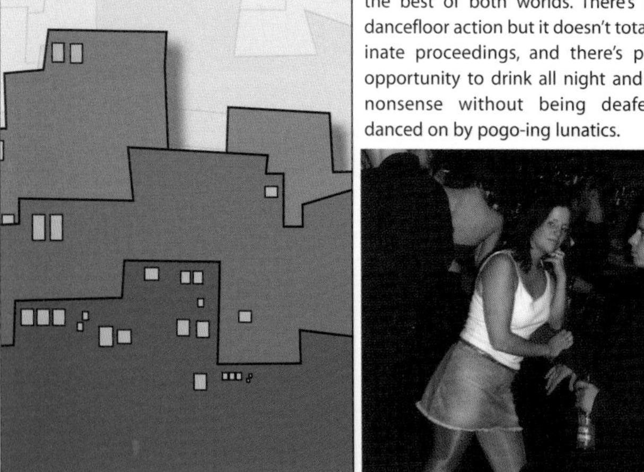

Beatroot

6-8 Broadway, The Lace Market
(0115) 924 0852

Like a longstanding resident of a recently gentrified neighbourhood, Beatroot has seen itself climb the social ladder as a by-product of the Lace Market regeneration. Time was you could pole up to the 'troot in your industrial work clothes and still be reluctant to lean on anything for fear of sticking to it. After investing a bit of cash in some new dusters, the club has understandably expected the crowd to follow suit and smarten their act up a bit. Proper shoes and smart casual clothing is advisable on Friday or Saturday nights despite my protestations that everyone's wearing Dunlop Green Flash and cut-off denims in London. As well as the refurbishment of the two main rooms, a new bar area was opened on the ground floor providing the perfect place to chill out when the funky house and R'n'B dominated dancefloors get too mashing.

The Bomb

45 Bridlesmith Gate (0115) 9506667

Still Nottingham's top dance club in my book (this one), the Bomb manages to maintain its popularity by finding the right balance between an underground music policy and a laid back attitude. You wont get over-hyped and over-payed house music DJs like Dan Santhams and Mick Selector playing here, but you will find top guests like Andy Wetherall and Andy Smith making regular appearances. The eclectic music and innovative booking policy has seen The Bomb responsible for bringing the likes of Prime Cuts and the Plump DJs to Nottingham for rare Midlands appearances. The venue itself is almost entirely white and is just the right size to generate an intimate but buzzing atmosphere. With 2 main rooms, 3 bars and access to Barrio's and the courtyard next door, The Bomb is also the ideal club for those with itchy feet or short attention spans.

The Cookie Club

9 Pelham Street (0115) 947 6136

A bit like having your end of term party in someone else's house: you can get pissed-up on cider and make a tit of yourself but you don't have to worry about cleaning the carpet tomorrow. Small and pretty dingy, The Cookie Club doesn't hold much appeal for the rising ranks of Nottingham's elitist bar dwellers, but it manages to just about get by without them, thanks all the same.

Hot tip

Dubble Bubble

19 Greyhound Street (0115) 952 0021

Not in fact a three way sexual act as the name might suggest, Dubble Bubble is actually a 2-floored club with a predominantly funk and hip-hop music policy. In these days of multi-million pound superclubs, this is a refreshingly rickety and somewhat dingy venue. There's no PlayStation IIs in the chill out room, and they're obviously still waiting to take delivery of the global satellite link up system, but in the meantime the crowd'll just have to entertain themselves with those outdated concepts like listening to a DJ who's actually in the same room and propping up the bar necking JD and Cokes.

Tom, 24, Barfly

What are your interests?
Hip Hop
And what's the best bar in town?
Broadway's cool, this place (Eleven) seems alright too.
And for the best club?
The Bomb is exactly that
What about something to eat?
Harts
And for shopping
Selectadisc
What's great about Nottingham?
All day sessions
And what's not?
Pretentious tossers

Edge

126 Lower Parliament Street (0115) 9413 338

Since it opened, towards the end of 2000, Edge has established itself as a genuine alternative for the city's clubbers. It perhaps hasn't had the same piles of cash poured into it as other recent additions to Nottingham's club scene, but the clean and minimal décor serve the purpose more than adequately. The bar area and downstairs dancefloor have a combined capacity of around 400, creating an intimate atmosphere with the emphasis on musical diversity. Thankfully, rather than just providing another stop on the big name DJ merry-go-round, Edge has adopted a policy of highlighting underground and up-and-coming talent. This stance is illustrated by the line-ups, with the likes of T Power and Freq Nasty headlining, rather than the usual suspects from the house circuit. Saturdays do have an electronica and Nu Skool breaks influence,

but the musical direction is too diverse to try and pigeonhole into single categories, as you can expect to hear house beats and straight-ahead techno as well. Friday nights work on a rotation system, first Friday of the month being Fusion's techno night, the second Friday drum 'n' bass from Fly, third Friday finds Hard8 in residence for hard house and trance, and the fourth Friday of the month is Smokescreen, a night of deep house. A new night for Thursdays is Call yourself a DJ, an opportunity for all bedroom turntablists to battle it out on the wheels of steel, with the possible prize of a weekend slot for the best spinners. Wannabe DJs should send a tape and contact number to the club.

Faces

The Broadway (0115) 958 9000

I don't actually own a copy, so I couldn't tell you on which page of the PFA players' handbook it states that upon visiting Nottingham, all professional footballers must converge on Faces nightclub, but it's definitely in there. Personally, I wouldn't show my arse in here never mind my face, but that probably comes as a relief to all concerned. However if you're over thirty and under the influence then this is the club for you. With a certain amount more sophistication than the corporate cattle markets, Faces attracts the kind of people with more cash to splash than aftershave, and that's saying something. Somewhat life-affirmingly, it also

Flick through the papers

goes to show that, plied with enough rum and coke, respectable middle class people are just as capable of making tools of themselves as the rest of us.

The Irish Centre

2-4 Wilford Street (0115) 947 3424

A dress code that clearly stipulates pants must be worn on head and trousers around ankles is usually confirmation of student club status. Whilst impromptu full monties are actually a rarity, the kind of high jinks usually associated with partying students is commonplace here, and that means shambolic dancing, desperate gropings, and the knobheads from the hockey club annoying everyone with their inability to hold their drink. The music policy works on the principle that if everyone's pissed enough they'll just about dance to anything, and they do.

Isis

Redfield Road, Lenton (0115) 986 3211

Underground clubs come and go, musical tastes change, scenes 'evolve'. And whilst all that nonsense goes on, corporate clubs like Isis still pack 'em in week after week. To say there's one in every city would be untrue (there's actually four), and there's good reason why these monolithic dance meccas plough on year after year in one form or another whilst 'cooler' clubs fall by the wayside: people love them. Isis delivers exactly what a lot of folk want: drinking, dancing, and the promise of a bit of a grapple, and if it didn't, people wouldn't bother making the effort to cart their denim-free arses out to this out of town venue.

Lizard Lounge

41-43 St Mary's Gate, The Lace Market (0115) 910 0300

Eternally popular club, attracting a healthy mix of a young fashion-conscious crew and a fair few of the more mature movers and moneyed shakers around town. Big queues are a regular sight, even on Thursday nights, let alone Friday or Saturday. With a strict dress policy enforced it's advisable to make something of an effort or risk the ignominity of exclusion. Downstairs is a bar and lounge area, and whilst upstairs you'll find some R 'n' B dancefloor action there is still plenty of space to lounge around looking all suave and seductive like.

Lost Weekend

169 Huntingdon Street (0115) 958 7071

Decent medium-sized venue on the outskirts of the city centre, The Lost Weekend has built a reputation in recent times as possibly the best club in town for house heads;

having staged some of the most outrageous and up for it nights that Nottingham has seen lately. There's been some coming and goings around the time of writing, with promoters moving on and new people moving in, but it's fair to assume that many of the loyal crowd will remain and ensure some level of continued popularity.

The Market Bar

16-22 Goose Gate, Hockley
(0115) 959 9777

An underground club, in the literal sense of the word, the Market Bar is a luxuriously-styled intimate cellar venue. In fact it's so modestly sized that given its popularity, it's almost impossible not to get pretty intimate with the other patrons (well that's my excuse, and I'm sticking to it). The music policy follows a fairly safe funk and house path and a large portion of the crowd are apparently here as much for posing as they are for serious dancefloor action.

Media

The Elite Building, Queen Street
(0115) 910 1101

There was a time that only mainstream clubs of the ilk of the Ritzy or MGM's could support a cast of thousands, but the recent phenomenon of the 'Superclub' has purported to bring the sound of the underground to a mass market. Bollocks of course. Superclubs are just the Ritzy of the 21st century and you're no more likely to hear the cutting edge of dance music here than you are listening to Dave Pearce's Dance Anthems show. This however is totally irrelevant, house music is irrefutably overground these days and Media is supplying the kids with their weekly fix of the 4/4 beats. Whilst the music policy in this impressively converted theatre is unquestionably dominated by house and its sub genres, there are certain nights like the monthly Soul when R'n'B or other musical styles get to takeover the dancefloors. The club also incorporates the highly exclusive Suede bar, which upon entry entitles you to rub shoulders with no less than a bloke who works in a clothes shop and the Saturday girl from a trendy hairdressers. Wow.

top 5 for...
places to pull

1. The Works
2. Ocean
3. The Palais
4. Isis
5. The Zone

Ocean

Greyfriar Gate (0115) 9411941

Your average member of the sub-forties population is driven by an innate desire to get laid, get ratted, and get their arses shaking to that record that goes 'da-da da-na na-na' every weekend, and whilst clubs like Ocean can't absolutely guarantee the former, two out of three ain't bad, as Meatloaf once said (I've just blown my street cred, haven't I?).

The Palais

Lower Parliament Street (0115) 950 1075

Corporate clubbing for the masses. Not my scene but then again I'm neither a rug-chested cheese merchant nor a shag-starved slapper (debatable – Ed). Most of you will either have been to the Palais or somewhere very similar before, and if you're into swaggering around to commercial dance music whilst getting utterly mullered, and are of an 'if it moves, shag it' mentality, then you'll be going back regardless of what I say. What, even with your buckled shoes, chino's, pink shirts, boob tubes etc etc.

Rock City

8 Talbot Street (0115) 950 2303

Buff up that medallion and grease down those leather pants, it's time to rock. Irrefutably one of the best rock clubs in the country, this huge venue is regularly packed to the rafters with rock chicks and cock-rock love gods on Saturday nights. Whilst the main room does indeed look like a Spinal Tap convention, the alternative music policy of the second room ensures that you get wannabe Fred Dursts mixing shoulders with Bernard St Hubbins look-alikes. One policy that is arbitrarily employed in both rooms is that the amps should indeed be turned up to 11, so earplugs might be advisable if you're planning on listening to anything other than dull distant ringing for the following week and a half. The venue also incorporates the adjacent Rig club, which generally caters for a more mainstream and party-conscious crowd.

The Works

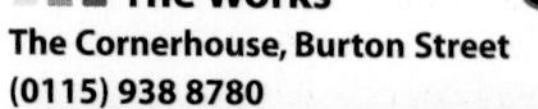

The Cornerhouse, Burton Street (0115) 938 8780

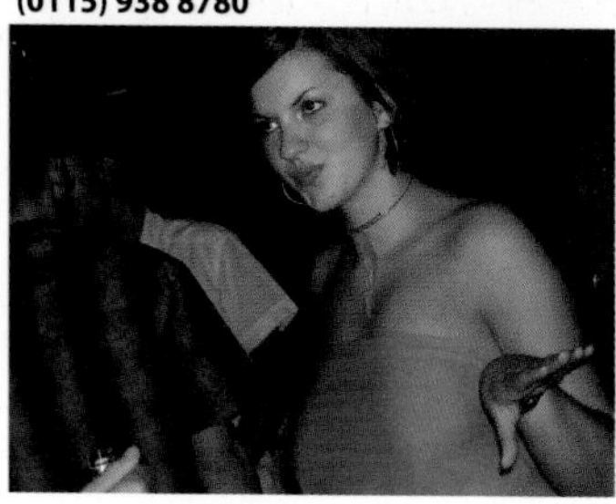

It's only appropriate that the Cornerhouse, Nottingham's newest and most impressive entertainment complex, should house the city's biggest and most ambitious nightclub. The Works is Nottingham's largest single club venue with a capacity of over 2000. The club itself is divided into two main rooms, with the first being predominantly dedicated to commercial dance and house music, and the second room generally taking a more staple party music path. Another major feature that separates the Works from most clubs is the bar area, which is open for normal trading hours throughout the week and offers some pretty decent food. In addition to this the main dance rooms are also open every evening from Monday to Sunday. Seven days a week dancefloor action may be great news for Nottingham's hardcore clubbers but I'm not sure how well it'll go down with the city's major employees. Just remember you've got work tomorrow. Oh sod it. Get the beers in.

The Zone

King Edward Street (0115) 950 1075

When Tiger Woods talks about being 'in the zone' I presume he doesn't mean here. Even at the height of its recent popularity as a full on baggy-panted indie club, the tell tale signs of its discorama history were barely suppressed. Recent times have seen the ghost of gorgonzola past resurface and gradually repossess the whole club again, meaning mop topped 'Mondays' fans are left to cry in their beer whilst the Bee Gees, Duran Duran and Robbie Williams all vie for dancefloor supremacy.

Best places for...

Techno, electronica
The Bomb, Edge

Jazz, soul, funk
Market Bar, Lizard Lounge, The Social

House, garage
Media, Edge, The Bomb, Beatroot

Indie
Cookie Club, Rock City, The Rig

Hip-hop, r'n'b, breaks
The Bomb, Dubble Bubble

World music, folk
Cuba Libra

Drum and bass
Edge, Dubble Bubble, The Bomb

Sixties, motown, northern soul
The Social, The Cookie Club

70s, 80s, disco
The Zone, The Works,

Pop, rock
Rock City, The Rig

Classical, opera
The Royal Concert Hall

Metal, alternative
Rock City, The Rig

Craig David
National Ice Centre

club listings

For more up-to-date reviews, previews and listings check www.itchynottingham.co.uk

All listings details are subject to change at short notice, and should therefore be used as a guide only. Basically, don't come knocking at my door when you go to a trance night and the place is full of goths sacrificing chickens and swinging their black pants to She Sells Sanctuary. OK?

Club	Night	Music	Door Tax	Close	Dress Code
MONDAY					
Isis	Juicy	House	£3	2am	No trainers
Lost Weekend		R 'n' B, soul		2am	Smartish
The Rig	Planet Earth	80's	£3/2 NUS	2am	No DC
The Works	-	Dance and chart.	free	12am	Smart casual
TUESDAY					
Lizard Lounge	Student	R n B, soul, garage	£2 NUS	2am	No DC
Lost Weekend	NCN Student	Dance and party music		2am	No DC
Market Bar	-	House and garage	£3/2 with flyer	2.30am	No DC
The Works	-	Dance and chart.	£4/3 members/itchy card	2am	Smart casual
Ocean	Student	Dance and chart.	£3 NUS	2am	Smart casual
The Palais	Student night	Dance and chart.	Free B4 11 - NUS, £2 after	-	-
WEDNESDAY					
Beatroot		Bhangra	£7/5	2am	No DC
Cuba Libra	Salsa Classes	Salsa & chart		2am	No DC
Lizard Lounge	Faster Pussycat	70's, 80's, 90's	£4/3	2am	No DC
Lost Weekend	Soul Society	R 'n' B, soul		2am	Smart casual
Market Bar	Live jazz	Jazz	£3/2 with flyer	2.30am	No DC
The Works		Dance and chart.	Tbc	2am	Smart casual
THURSDAY					
Beatroot	Babes in Toyland	House	£5/3 NUS	2am	funky
Bomb	Bring da Noize (fortnightly)	Hip Hop	£5	3am	No DC
Cuba Libra	Salsa Classes	Salsa & chart		2am	No DC
Cookie Club	Up the Junction	60's-90's	£2/1.50 NUS	2am	No DC
Faces	Ladies night	80s/90s	£3/2	2am	No trainers
Edge	Call yourself a DJ?	Wannabe DJs play their own vinyl	-	2am	No DC
Lizard Lounge	That's Right	House, funk, R 'n' B, pop	£3	2am	Smart casual
Lost Weekend	Sound Kartel	Hip Hop, jazzy breaks		2am	Smart casual
The Palais	VFM (cheap drinks)	Commercial dance and chart.	£3/1 with flyer	2am	smart
The Rig	Damaged	Metal	£3/2 B4 11	2am	No DC
Rock City	Tuned (student)	Indy rock and pop	£2.50/£1.50 NUS	2am	No DC
The Works		Dance and chart.	£4/3 members/itchy card	2am	Smart casual
The Zone	Loaded	Dance and pop	£4	2am	No DC

Take a leaf out of our book

FRIDAY

Cookie Club	Retro	60s-90s	£4/£3 NUS	2am	No DC
Bomb	Alternates between: Tyrant. Breakdown. DIY Insight	Tech House. Breaks. Deep House Drum n bass.	£7-9	3am	No DC
Dubble Bubble		Funk, beats, breaks	£3 members/NUS, £4 others	2am	No DC
Edge	Alternates between:	House. Techno. Drum n bass. Hard House	£6	3am	No DC
Faces	-	Commercial dance and chart	£5/3 B4 11	2am	smart
Irish	Student night	Indy dance and chart	£2	2am	No DC
Isis	-	Chart and dance	£4 B4 11, £5 after		No T-shirts, trainers or denim
Lizard Lounge	-	Dance, garage, funk, RnB	£5	2am	Smart/Fashionable
Lost Weekend	Motion	Deep progressive house		2am	clubwear
Market Bar	-	House, breaks, funky beats	£3 after 10pm	2am	Smart casual
Ocean	-	Chart and commercial	£1 B4 11, £2 after		No blue denim or trainers
Palais	Fun	Party music	£5 B4 11, £6 after	2am	No blue denim or trainers
The Works	-	-	£7/6 members/itchycard	3am	Smart casual
The Zone	Student night	Indie, dance	Free B4 11 with NUS, £2 after	2am	No DC

SATURDAY

Beatroot	-	Funky house and dance	£3	2am	Smart casual
The Bomb	Drop the Bomb	Tech House, funk, soul	£10/8 members/NUS	3am	No DC
Cookie Club	Rise and Shine	Indy, big beat	£4/3 NUS	2am	No DC
Dubble Bubble	Vibe	Funk	£5 members/NUS, £6 others	2am	Casual
Edge	-	House, breaks, techno.	£6/5 members	3am	No DC
Faces	-	Commercial dance	£8/6 members	2am	No trainers or jeans.
Irish	Student night	Indy dance and chart	£2	2am	No DC
Isis	-	Chart and dance	£5 B4 11, £7 after		No T-shirts, trainers or denim
Lizard Lounge	-	Dance, garage, funk, RnB	£5	2am	Smart/fashionable
Lost Weekend	Love Zoo	Funky House		2am	Clubwear
Market Bar	-	House, breaks, funky beats	£3 after 10pm	2.30am	Smart casual
Media	Renaissance	House	£12/10 members/NUS	3am	Smart casual.
Ocean	Seduction	Commercial dance	£6/4	2am	No blue denim or trainers
Palais	-	Commercial dance	£7	2am	No trainers or blue denim
The Works	-		£4/3 members/itchy card	3am	Smart casual
The Zone	-	Anything goes	£2	2am	£2 all drinks. No DC

SUNDAY

Old Vic	Just the Tonic	Comedy Club	£7/5. £1 off with itchy card	7.30-12	No DC
The Works	-	Commercial dance	Free B4 10.30	1am	Smart casual

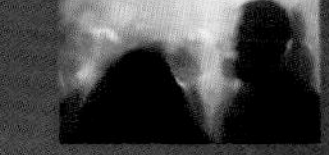

shopping

www.itchynottingham.co.uk

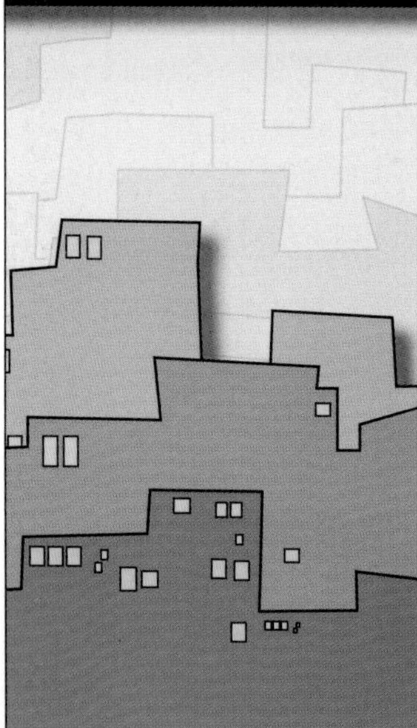

Spend a few hours (and a few pounds) around Nottingham's city centre and you'll soon see why it has had a reputation as something of a fashion centre for many years. Obviously one name is synonymous with Nottingham fashion, but a quick look down Bridlesmith Gate will be enough to assure you that Paul Smith isn't the be all and end all. Be warned, even though it's predominantly chain stores, a lot of the Bridlesmith Gate gear can be pretty pricey, so reckless use of the plastic could leave your wallet in need of some serious CPR. If Prada or DKNY aren't your bag then there's plenty of independent clothes shops in Hockley, where the emphasis is on street style and the damage to your bank balance shouldn't be terminal.

Department Stores

Alders

7 Broad Marsh Centre (0115) 912 6000

One of the better things in the Broad Marsh, this department store has everything from pots and pans to socks and smalls.

House of Fraser

2 Union Road (0115) 911 5511

Big department store attached to the Victoria Centre. Upmarket as department stores go, and particularly good for designer label clothes.

Jessop and Son

175-182 Victoria Centre (0115) 941 8282

Called John Lewis's now but this long-standing department store will always be Jessops to Nottingham folk. Household appliances, kitchenware, fabrics and more.

Shopping Centres

The Broad Marsh Centre

Canal Street (0115) 840 4555

Utterly bog-standard shopping centre in dire need of regeneration. There's a pretty decent sized Boots chemist, an Alders and a Works bookshop, but other than that it's mostly cheap pound shops and stationers. However mediocre the shopping area may be though, it's truly glamorous in comparison to the connected bus station. Grim beyond belief, it's distinguished by the dubious honour of having possibly the most disgusting toilets in the Midlands. It's advisable to avoid altogether, but if you do venture in, it's essential to dodge the discarded hypodermics and occasional dead bodies scattered about. Truly sinister.

Open for access 6.30am-6.30pm Mon-Sat 10am-5pm Sun
Shops open 8.30/9am-5.30pm Mon-Sat 10.30am-4.30pm Sun

Exchange Arcade

Exchange Buildings, Smithy Road (0115) 947 0591

In utter contrast to 90 percent of modern shopping centres, the rather classy Exchange Arcade is a tasteful haven from the city centre streets. Being predominantly filled with clothing stores from the higher end of the market, it's popular with those looking for a bit more grown-up style than the high street. Some of it's a bit pricey, but if you're going to be restricted to window shopping you may as well do it somewhere with good air conditioning.

Mon-Sat 9.30am-5.30pm except Wed 'til 8pm. Sun 11am-4pm

Flying Horse Shopping Centre

South Parade (0115) 948 4926

Hardly a shopping centre, this is more a small number of mostly specialist shops. If you're after some ornate glasswork or an objet d'art for your mum's birthday then you

might want to make the Flying Horse Arcade your first port of call. A bit old and fuddy duddy, but then again, so's your mum.

Mon-Sat 9-5.30. Open Sundays in run up to Christmas.

Kings Walk

Ignore Broad Marsh and the high street, and head down towards Kings Walk for the cooler alternative to shopping in Nottingham. Shops include Julieann Eve, Long Tall Sally, The Little London Herbal Store and the superb Petit Paris restaurant. You'll find it situated between Upper Parliament Street and the Cornerhouse development.

Victoria Centre

Milton Street (0115) 912 1111

Slightly bigger than the Broad Marsh, and slightly less crap, it has most of the shops you'd expect of a typical shopping centre: HMV, WHSmiths, Top Shop and Next.

Mon-Fri 9-5.30 (late night Wed 'til 7.30). Sat 9-6pm Sun 10.30-4.30

Men's

Boxer Clothing

King John's Arcade (0115) 950 0170

Cool independent clothes shop that's worth seeking out. Boxer carries a load of top labels like Sharpeye, Burro, Red Dot, Seal Kay, and DKNY Jeans. A big plus with smaller shops like this is that you don't have to deal with clueless Saturday staff or pretentious assistant trainee managers in waiting; the only person who works here is the owner, a decent guy who knows what he's talking about.

Crow & Jester

16-22 Goosegate (0115) 950 4950

Cool independent menswear shop specialising in high quality tailored suits.

Jaeger Man

Within House of Fraser, 2 Union Road (0115) 912 1323

Who is Jaeger man? He's the guy in the beige linen suit drinking martinis on the patio by the swimming pool. No, he's not me either.

Reiss

5 Byard Lane (0115) 950 1025

Sartorial elegance abounds at this cool and spacious Reiss. Simple, stylish clothes.

Paul Smith

10 Byard Lane (0115) 950 6712

Well it's Paul Smith innit? Famous throughout the world but Nottingham's where it all began for the coolest name in British fashion. Striking the right balance between traditional tailoring and street style, the shop is pleasantly laid back and unintimidating. The staff are casually dressed and attitude free, and happy to let you browse away. Even if you can't afford one of the famous suits, the

range of T-shirts and jeans aren't as pricey as you might fear.

Women's Clothing

Coast
24 Bridlesmith Gate (0115) 941 7466
It's mostly pretty simple stuff but often quite nice. Particularly good for summery clothes.

Jigsaw
Bridlesmith Gate (0115) 941 4437
Excellent own brand clothing, simple and stylish. And there's a café downstairs.

Karen Millen
15 Exchange Arcade (0115) 947 2829
Cool modern and friendly women's clothing store that doesn't try to be overly trendy.

Milli
Queen Street (0115) 950 2882
Smart women's clothes shop close to market square. Chloe, Marni, Miu Miu and Paul Smith women.

Reiss
5 Byard Lane (0115) 950 1025
Top quality stylish clothes store with a surprisingly large women's section in the basement area (that's a surprisingly large section, not a section for surprisingly large women).

Unisex

Birdcage
20 Carlton Street, (0115) 941 4204
Smart and casual streetwear and accessories. Ladies on the ground floor, gents upstairs.

G Force
Carlton Street, Hockley (0115) 911 2078
I'll take a neon-white lycra catsuit with matching cape, and one of those space helmets with the eagle's beak visors please. What do you mean you only sell modern urban casual clothing? (the last obscure 70's Japanese cartoon reference, promise.)

PLAN YOUR RESIGNATION TACTICALLY

Loud

Designers Studios, 69-73 Lower Parliament Street (0115) 950 6050

Tucked away from the main shopping areas, but well worth seeking out for those special occasions. Mostly one-off items and outfits with a touch of glamour. Specialising in clubwear and ball-gowns. Any size, any occasion, and created just for you.

HSC

Carlton Street, Hockley (0115) 941 8070

Quality shop with loads of top skate and streetwear. Good selection of T-shirts, trainers and baggy pants for people who say dude a lot.

Speedo Shop

South Parade

It was to the relief of a generation of teenage boys that the pre-eminence of old school Speedo's dissipated in the mid-eighties to be usurped by the modesty-preserving Bermuda short. Well they're back. The thought may induce flashbacks of towel fights and diving for rubber bricks, but Speedos have grown up even if you haven't. They still do the classic trunk for those of a Mediterranean extraction, but the rest of us can now choose from an altogether more appropriate selection of swimwear. Unfortunately they don't sell any of those fluorescent duffel bags with pictures of footballers on. (Come on, you remember them.)

REMEMBER, LEAVE ON A POSITIVE NOTE.

Urban Myth

Carlton Street, Hockley (0115) 941 5063

A friend of a friend once bought a pair of imported South American trousers from here that had a spider's nest in the gusset. The eggs hatched when he was wearing them and all the baby spiders climbed up his arse and he didn't realise until tarantulas started coming out of his nose. This of course is not true. What it does in fact sell is reasonably priced streetwear from labels like Duck and Cover.

Uth

26-28 Bridlesmith Gate (0115) 9581521

Large and modern Bridlesmith Gate clothes shop. Most of the clothes are quite simple and stylish and go from very affordable tops and T-shirts right up to some pretty spicy suits and jackets. Some of the staff look like they take it a bit too seriously but they're probably a bit confused about the name change (Uth being the new name for Jigsaw menswear).

Shoes

Sole

Bridlesmith Gate (0115) 840 2700

Manages to carry one of the best selections of footwear in town despite being little bigger than a shoebox itself.

soletrader

44 Bridlesmith Gate 0115 924 0111

Ideally located in the heart of Nottingham's trendiest shopping area, this newcomer looks like a particularly vivid scene from an Imelda Marcos erotic dream. Absolutely shed loads of wicked shoes from the top brands: Camper, Nike, Diesel etc.

Solution
Pelham Street (0115) 956 7005
Slightly larger sister shop to Sole and with a similarly good selection of foot clobber.

Record Shops

Funky Monkey
14 Goosegate (0115) 9561181
Small independent record shop that carries a good selection of vinyl covering styles from house, garage, hip hop, R'n'B, techno, and drum'n'bass to name but six. There's also none of the superior elitist attitude you get in some specialist shops.

HMV
38 Listergate (0115) 950 2662
134 Victoria Centre (0115) 941 5525
Any shop that has a section, no matter how small, dedicated solely to Botchit & Scarper records is all right in my book. Of course there's loads of stuff that people actually buy as well, and a good selection of videos, DVDs and computer games.

Robs Records
Hurts Yard
Proper second-hand vinyl shop. Racks of wax and crates of greats (and some not so greats) from all styles and all years.

Selectadisc
3 and 19-21 Market Street
(0115) 941 7166/947 5420
This has to be one of the best recorc. .hops in England, let alone Nottingham. With three shops in total (two having recently been combined) catering for a wide variety of styles, selling singles, albums, second hand records and even clothing, you could be missing for hours. It's especially good for the vinyl junkie with rows and rows of wax including hip hop, house, techno, and electronica you'll be a bedroom DJ in no time at all.

Virgin Megastore
6 Wheeler Gate (0115) 947 6126
Huge two-floored store with boat-loads of CDs, videos, computer games, books and magazines. There's also a reasonable selection of vinyl.

Bookshops

Forbidden Planet

129 Middle Walk, Broad Marsh Centre
(0115) 958 4706

Massive selection of fantasy and science fiction related books, comics and games.

Waterstone's

1/5 Bridlesmith Gate (0115) 948 4499

The biggest and best bookstore in town. Five floors comprising of an exhibition area, an espresso bar and of course racks and racks of books on almost any subject you could be looking for.

Waterstone's

25 Wheeler Gate (0115) 947 3531

Not as swanky as the flagship store on Bridlesmith Gate but still good.

WHATEVER TURNS YOU ON
Virgin
megastores

cool modern furniture and items for your loft style apartment.

Luna

23 George Street (0115) 924 3267

Cool retro gifts from the last millennium. Old toys, cigarette lighters and the odd juke-box.

Josiah Brown

7 Market Street (0115) 941 7308

Smoking is not good for you. It is cool though, and if you're planning to start, start here. The best selection of cigars and snuff in the city.

WHSmiths

14-6 Listergate (0115) 958 2919

It's not a library you know. Massive Smiths that fills all your magazine, newspaper and stationery requirements as well having a good selection of books, videos and CDs.

WHSmiths

124-126 Victoria Centre (0115) 978 3567

Smaller of the two city centre Smiths, but still a good selection of magazines, papers, books and more.

The Works

55 Broad Walk, The Broad Marsh Centre (0115) 950 9217

Wide variety of budget priced books.

Other Cool Shops

Atomic

Plumptre Square, The Lace Market (0115) 924 3267

Ideally located on the fringes of the Lace Market, this big brother to the King John's shop is a larger showroom that specialises in

Claire, 20, Student

Favourite place for a drink?
It was here (the Social)
What about a bite to eat?
Jigsaw
I think you'll find that's a clothes shop.
I think *you'll* find it's a café too.
So what's your favourite shop then, Caffé Uno?
Very funny. It's Jigsaw of course.
That figures. So what's the best thing about Nottingham? Jigsaw perhaps?
You're starting to annoy me.
Worst thing about Nottingham?
Do you really want me to answer that.

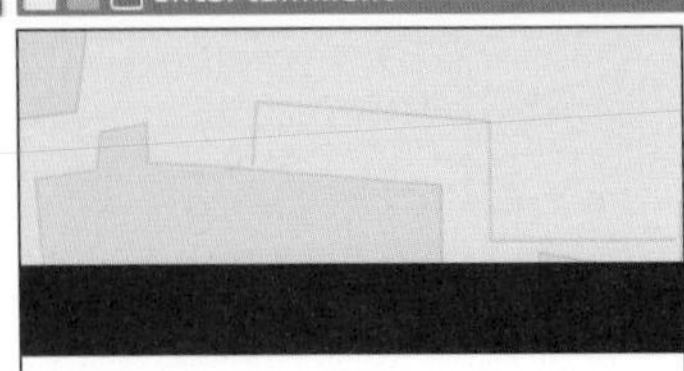

entertainment

www.itchynottingham.co.uk

Cinemas

Broadway

14-16 Broad Street (0115) 952 6611 info (0115) 952 6600 box office.

Cool cinema showing alternative and independent films and some of the more interesting mainstream releases.

Prices £4.20/3.10 concessions

Savoy

233 Derby Road (0115) 947 2580

Traditional old cinema on the outskirts of the city centre.

£4 adults. £3 concessions

Showcase

Redfield Way, Lenton Industrial Estate (0115) 986 6766

Huge multiplex cinema, specialising in American historical documentaries. You know the ones where they win all the wars and save the planet through a combination of computer generated imagery and clichéd dialogue.

Prices from £4

Warner Village

The Cornerhouse, Forman Street
(0115) 950 0135 card bookings

Impressive looking cinema that forms the focal point of the cornerhouse development.

Adults £5.50 concessions £4

Theatres

Nottingham Playhouse

Wellington Circus (0115) 948 2525 (credit card booking line) 0115 947 4361

Smaller independent productions are staged in this repertory theatre. Recent shows have included 'Travels with my Aunt' and 'Dick Barton – Special Agent' but the shows are generally very varied.

The Theatre Royal

The Royal Centre (0115) 989 5555

Larger touring shows including many straight from the West End, such as Jesus Christ Superstar.

Live Music

Damn that boy can sing. You must be crazy. A whole host of Nottingham bars and pubs have live music but in terms of 'proper' gigs there's only a limited number of serious venues. The Ice Centre is the only place even approaching arena status and consequently attracts the bigger names from the world of pop. Traditionally, Nottingham's top venue is Rock City but don't let the name fool you - you're more likely to hear Ian Brown than

David Coverdale, and a good atmosphere is usually guaranteed. For details of up and coming events and gigs, check www.itchynottingham.co.uk.

Berlins

1 Hockley (0115) 948 1899

Don't let the music interrupt your drinking.

Katmandu

Old Bus Depot, Mansfield Road, Sherwood (0115) 911 1910

There are often live jazz bands in this impressive bar venue.

The National Ice Centre

Lower Parliament Street
Box Office (0115) 853 3000

Nottingham's biggest venue for live music. Attracts big names like Tom Jones, Craig David, and Roxy Music.

Rock City

8 Talbot Street (0115) 9412544
(0115) 9588484 credit card hotline

Long-standing venue that gets plenty of big name bands that aren't quite at the arena tour level. A really good atmosphere for the best gigs, with crowd surfing and everything. Cool man.

Royal Concert Hall

The Royal Centre (0115) 989 5555

A wide range of concerts from classical and opera to Daniel O'Donnell.

The Social

23 Pelham Street (0115) 950 5078

Not much bigger than your living room but they get some pretty cool bands. Has recently been home to nights with Starsailor, Ed Harcourt and the Stereo MCs.

Sugar Bar

Broadway, The Lace Market
(0115) 947 5083

Different live Salsa bands every Wednesday.

Comedy Clubs

Details of comedy nights can be found at **www.itchynottingham.co.uk**

Jongleurs

British Waterways Building
020 7564 2500 (any Jongleurs venue)

Enjoy the big names from the world of comedy, then stick around and give everyone a good laugh on the dancefloor as the venue becomes a nightclub.

Just the Tonic

The Old Vic, Fletcher Gate
Info (0115) 910 0009

Best of the comedy circuit every Sunday

IT'S THE MD

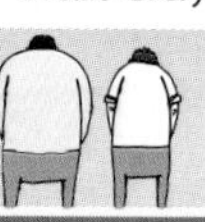

night. The big names in comedy have all appeared here and they keep coming back. This night has a truly underground and alternative feel. People that know comedy go to Just the Tonic… quality line-ups, cheap entry, pub price drinks, bar until 12.
Ticket prices £7 (£5 concessions)
£1 off with itchy card

Sport

Nottingham Forest

Pavillion Road, West Bridgford
(0115) 982 4444
Ticket Office (0115) 982 4445

After some turbulent years of yo-yoing, Forest now appear to have found a level of consistency. Unfortunately that level is the First Division. Another summer of turmoil has seen the much maligned David Platt move on to the England U21 role, and Forest's own youth team coach Paul Hart promoted to the top job.There may not be a Stan Collymore or a Pierre van Hooijdonk at the club anymore, but for the first time in years, young home grown players are starting to breakthrough. If anyone can oversee their progress, and translate the success of the academy to the first team, then Paul Hart should be the man. With the likes of Jermaine Jenas and Eugen Bopp knocking on the dressing room door to join Prutton, Doig, Williams, Edds and Foy in the first team squad then the Reds could be pushing for a promotion spot by the time you read this.

top 5 for...
watch the footy

1. Southbank Bar
2. Hooters
3. The Park
4. Byrons
5. Fellows

Notts County FC

Meadow Lane (0115) 9529000
Ticket Office (0115) 95 57210

After a promising first season under the stewardship of Jocky Scott, there's an air of optimism around Meadow Lane. They may have lost their goalkeeper to their bitter rivals across the Trent, but there was enough positive transfer activity over the summer to suggest a successful season for the Magpies. The signings of Darren Caskey and Tony Hackworth have signaled the ambition of the club and I expect them to be pushing for a play-off spot at least this season.

Nottinghamshire County Cricket Club

Trent Bridge, Bridgford Road, West Bridgford (0115) 982 1525
Ticket office (0115) 981 7005

Notts may be alarmingly inconsistent, but thanks to impressive recent development Trent Bridge remains established as one of the top test match venues in the country.

Karting

County Karting

Circuits at Fosseway and Leicester
0800 731 8666
Open 10-5.30
Outdoor karting, 12 laps £10, 20 laps £15

Stretton 2000

Leicester Airport, Great Stretton, Leicester (0116) 259 2900
Open 10am-6pm
15 minutes £20, 30 minutes £35

Paintball

Has Dave in accounts been pushing his luck? Sarah in the typing-pool been bitching about you again? It's payback time.

Skirmish

Site location Sherwood Forest
0800 328 2785
Full day £25-50 dependant on how many balls you have.
Mon-Fri 8am-9m. Sat-Sun 8.30-5,30pm

The Paintball Jungle

26 Galway Road, Arnold
0800 952 6272
10am-4pm
£15 per day, inc 100 paintballs

Golf

Indulge your suppressed desire to dress like Rupert the Bear for a couple of hours.

Nottingham City Golf Club

Lawton Lane, Bulwell (0115) 927 2767
First tee off at approximately 8.30am.
£11 per round Mon-Fri. £13 Sat-Sun

Trentside Golf Course

Trentside, Lenton Lane (0115) 9862179
£4.40 for 9 holes. £6.40 for 18 holes

Bowling

AMF

Bakergate House, Belward Street (0115) 950 5588
Adults: £1 shoe hire. £2.55 per game before 6pm, £3.40 after
Juniors: 60p shoe hire. £2.10 per game before 6pm

JUST KEEP SMILING AT HIM

Megabowl

Redfield Road (0115) 985 0820

Adults: 1 game £4.50. 2 games £8 3 games £9.50. Juniors: 1 game £3.50 2 games £6. 3 games £7.50 Mon-Thur 12am-11pm. Sat 10am-1am Sun 10am-11pm

Pool & Snooker

Q Lounge

Long Row (0115) 840 5472

Huge bar and American style pool hall. OK for a few frames in the afternoon, but I wouldn't undertake any 30 frame marathon grudge matches on Saturday night as the booming sound system's liable to bounce your balls right off the table.

Rileys Snooker Club

17a St James Street (0115) 914 5147

Open 24 hours, this is the most dedicated pool and snooker hall in the city.

Membership £5. Tables £4 p/h

Stadium Leisure Snooker

Nottingham road, New Basford (0115) 970 5523

Serious snooker hall for players of all standards, though expect to get plubered.

£10 membership. Tables £1.80 per hour before 5pm £3.60 after

The Spot On Club

Vine Terrace, Hucknall (0115) 964 1514

Another club for serious snooker heads.

Membership £5. Tables £2.30 before 5pm, £3.50 after

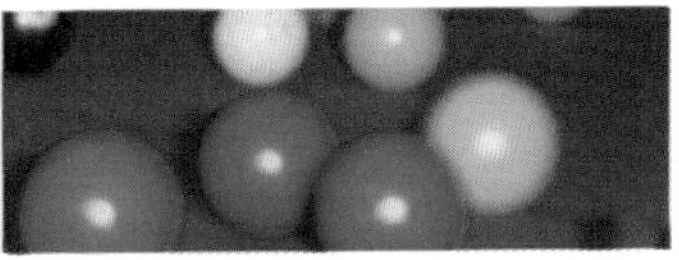

Casinos

Want to make sure you're 'Sitting with the nuts' on the river? Like to know how to represent Aces when holding the 'Gay waiter'? Then you need 'How to win at gambling'. For your copy of this indispensable guide please send £5 postal order to: Si Smith, C/board Box 4, Skid Row, Loserville, Notts.

Casino Club Nottingham

1-9 Bridlesmith Gate (0115) 958 1800

Mon-Sat 2pm-6am. Sun 2pm-4am

Regency Casino

4 Maid Marion Way (0115) 979 9288

Sun-Fri 5pm-6am. Sat 5pm-4am

MEGABOWL

Galleries and Museums

Angel Row Gallery

:entral Library Building, 3 Angel Row
0115) 915 2869

:lean modern space that predominantly lisplays modern art from both local and ıational talent.

Aon-Sat 10-5, Wed 10-7

Bonnington Gallery

Nottingham Trent University,
3onnington Building, Dryden Street
0115) 948 6433

Jsed for student graduation shows but here's also occasional exhibits from estab- 'shed artists from all fields of the arts.

'imes vary dependant on the time of year

Caves of Nottingham

3roadmarsh Centre (0115) 924 1424

No, not a guided tour of the drinking estab- ishments of Upper Parliament Street this is ın exploration of the actual underground 'ave networks that run under the city. 'opular with the kids there's also enough to :eep grown-ups happy and it's a definite ourist fave.

:3.25/2.25 NUS, OAP, child
Aon-Sat 10-4.15. Sun 11-4

Galleries of Justice

ligh Pavement (0115) 952 0555

o David Platt has walked out on the sham- ɔles he helped to create at Forest and traight into a multi-million pound job with he FA. Well this legally-themed attraction harks back to a time when there was justice in the world.

£6.95 adult, £5.95 concs, £22.95 family
Tues-Sat 9.30-4. Sun 10-4

Nottingham Castle Museum

Friar Lane (0115) 915 3700

Regular art exhibitions. Local and interna- tional artists showing a wide variety of works from photography to painting and sculptures.

10-5 everyday

Tales of Robin Hood

30-38 Maid Marion Way (0115) 948 3284

Not too bad really, we've gone nearly three quarters of the book without giving him a mention. A guided tour round a pseudo Sherwood Forest where you'll meet Robin Hood and his merry men (or at least some poor unfortunates who've had to struggle into a pair of Lincoln green leggings).

£4.95 adults, £3.95 children
10-6 everyday

Sherwood Forest

Tourist Information Centre
(01623) 823 202

You're not allowed to climb the Major Oak these days but it's still worth a trip.

body

www.itchynottingham.co.uk

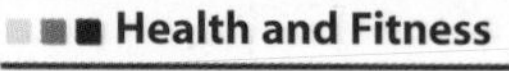

Health and Fitness

Castle Gym

4 Castle Boulevard (0115) 947 0319

Centrally located gym. No swimming pool o saunas but plenty of proper kit for seriou gym bods.

Prices from day £2.60, week £6, month £21 and year £150

Mon-Thu 10-9pm, Fri 10-8pm, Sat 10-2pm Sun 10-1pm

David Lloyd Leisure

Aspley Lane (0115) 900 7001

Full gym, sauna and leisure facilities in thi upmarket leisure and health centre.

Lifetime membership fee £230, then £54/month

Mon-Sun 7am-11pm

Fitness First

British Waterways Building, Castle Wharf (0115) 959 8222

Well-equipped gym on the top floor of th British Waterways Building. Full gymnasiur spa, sauna and sunbeds. The truly commit ted will take the stairs.

£33 month gold membership, £24 off-peak membership

Mon-Fri 6.30am-10pm, Sat 8am-9pm, Sun 8am-10pm

Formula One

21 Victoria Street (0115) 950 5009

Separate gymnasiums for male and femal members.

Joining fee £20 plus £195 annual membership 1 month/3 month/6 month membership also available

Mon-Fri 7am-11pm. Sat 9am-4pm, Sun 9-3pm

Holmes Place

Low Level Station, The Great Northern Close, London Road (0115) 988 4747

Impressive and large gym, full fitness facilities and a swimming pool. Just out of the city centre and with plenty of parking space. Various different membership packages and rates tailored to your individual needs. Ring for consultation.

Sat-Sun 9am-9pm Mon-Fri 6.30am-10pm

Lady in Leisure

Commercial House, Thurland Street (0115) 924 3636

Aerobics and sauna as well as full gymnasium facilities in this ladies only fitness centre.

£300 year
Mon-Sun 7am-9.30pm

Beauty

Thurland Street Beauty

8 Thurland Street (0115) 947 4702

Massage, facials, waxing and manicures.

£17 facial
Mon 9-6pm, Tue-Fri 9-7pm, Sat 8.30-5pm

Bodycare

62 Carlton Road, Carlton (0115) 940 3003

Hairdressing, beauty therapy and sunbeds.

Beauty therapy from £5.75
Mon 9-6pm, Tue-Fri 9.30-7pm, Sat 9.30-6pm

Complexions

1 Church Drive, Daybrook (0115) 9208144

Facials, massages, pedicure/manicure, body waxing, non-surgical facelifts, electrolysis, eyelash tinting and shaping. Non-surgical heaven for ugly people.

Facials from £30.50
Mon 9-9, Tue-Fri 9-7, Sat 9-5

Nev, old enough to be your dad, lecturer

So where do you sink the most vino?
Sinatra's.
And eat the most pies?
Harts.
Harts? Where do you spend the rest of my inheritance?
Waterstone's.
Could you lend m a tenner?
I'll lend you a bunch of fives in a minute.
Top of the class in Nottingham?
It's compact city centre.
Could do better?
Nowhere to socialise once you pass 21.

Tanning

Level 3
17 Long Row (0115) 924 1400
Fast tanning facilities with prices from £3 for 3 mins, ranging up to 3-hour course at £65.
Mon-Fri 10-5.30. Sat 10-5

Utopia Tanning
8 Broad Street, Hockley (0115) 941 3606
White's in. But if you don't care about fashion get yourself down to Utopia.
From 50p per minute. 3 hour courses £60
Mon-Thur 9-7. Fri 9-6. Sat 9-5

Tattooists and Piercings

Access All Areas Body Piercing
17a Market Street (0115) 941 9992
Piercing prices start from around **£4** depending on what you're getting pierced, naturally.
Mon-Sat 10-6 except Tues 10-5

Dannys Tattoo Studio
20 Southwell Road, Sneinton
(0115) 950 1505
Award winning tattoos.
Prices start at around £15
Mon-Fri 11-6. Sat 10-5

DC Tattoo Studio
23 St Christopher Street (0115 950 6830)
Specialising in one-off original pieces.
£35 per hour, plus charge for artwork
Mon-Fri 10.30-6 appointment only

Hairdressers

Unisex

Ann Martin
25-27 Bridlesmith Gate (0115) 941 0763
Ann chops mops.
Men from £21, women £27. 10% student discount Mon-Thu
Mon-Fri 9-6pm, Sat 9-5, Sun 10-4

Essensuals
5 Long Row (0115) 98 81777
Classy ladies and gents hairstylists.
Women £24-£35, men £22-£27
Mon-Fri 9-7pm, Sat 9-6pm

Surreal

8 Byard Lane (0115) 9582356

Also do nail manicures and therapeutics.

Women £24.50-£34.50, men £22.50-£30.50

Tues 10-6pm, Wed 10-7pm, Thu 9-5pm, Fri 10.30-6pm, Sat 9-5pm

Toni and Guy

4 Cheapside (0115) 9415756

Top class salon that's part of the national chain. Cuts, colouring and styling at a wide range of prices.

Cut and blow dry from £27.50

Mon-Fri 9-7pm, Sat 9-6pm

Mens

28 Goose Gate

28 Goose Gate, Hockley (0115) 958 6628

This modern and stylish take on the traditional barbers is one of the best around for a quality cut at a sensible price. It's now the only place in the region that offers a proper shaving service where you get the full VIP treatment: heated towels, facial massage, the whole bit. Class.

Gents dry £11, wet £13, NUS discount £2

Mon-Sat 9.30-6, late-night Wed

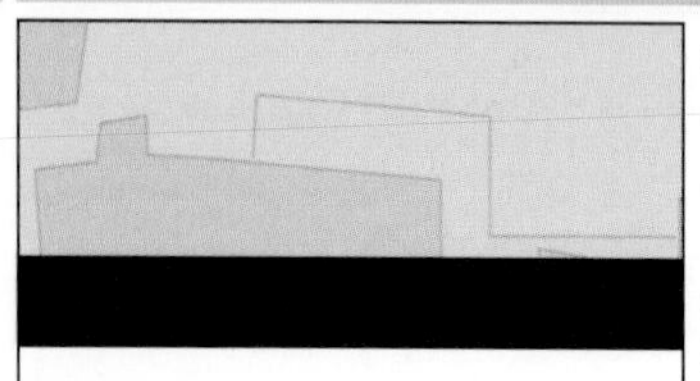

takeaway

www.itchynottingham.co.uk

No delivery unless otherwise stated.

Asian

Bombay Bicycle Shop

511 Alfreton Road (0115) 978 6309

Possibly the best takeaway curry in town. Open 'til 11pm for collection, no delivery orders taken after 10.30.
Delivery service.

Ghandi Indian Takeaway

36 Gordon Road, West Bridgeford (0115) 981 7532

Pretty good but it doesn't open very late. Open 'til 12.

Purnima

14 Musters Road, West Bridgeford (0115) 981 1712

Open 'til 12, closed Mondays.
Delivery service.

Sanam Tandoori

505 Mansfield Road (0115) 962 6563

Open 'til 12.
Delivery service.

Fish and Chips

Avenue Fish Bar

8b Central Avenue, West Bridgeford (0115) 914 0165

Not too bad.
Open 'til 11.

Eat Out Chip Shop

543 Mansfield Road (0115) 911 2064

...or eat in, the choice is yours.
Open 'til 11.

Harry Ramsden's
Riverside Park, Queens Drive
(0115) 986 1304
The idea of pre-cooking food for the lunchtime rush is a concept lost on the staff in here, but if you can bear the wait, it's the best F&Cs around.
Open 'til 10.30.

The Island Fish Bar
173 Nuthall Road (0115) 978 3869
Open 'til 10.30.

Wise Place
508 Carlton Road (0115) 950 5216
Open 'til 10.30.

Kebabs, burger and pizzas

Caspian Kebab House
36 Alfreton Road (0115) 978 4865
Open 'til 12.

Grab A Bite
276 Alfreton Road (0115) 841 4433
Open 'til 1am.

Falafel
9 Heathcote Street (0115) 988 1313
Open 'til 12. Delivery service.

Carringtons
89 Carrington Street (0115) 958 1881
Open 'til 12.

Pizza Stop
69 Mansfield Road (0115) 950 4565
Open 'til 5am Fri-Sat. 4am Mon-Thu
Delivery service.

Tastee Kebab
177 Alfreton Road (0115) 978 5710
Open 'til 3.30am. Delivery service.

Victoria Kebab House
39 Mansfield Road (0115) 950 6661
Open 'til 3am.

Oriental

Day & Night
1 Trent Boulevard, West Bridgeford
(0115) 982 0887
Don't rate it personally.
Open 'til 11.

Double Seven Cantonese
75 Melton Road, West Bridgeford
(0115) 981 6228
Absolutely top drawer. The exotic set menu for two is a Sunday night ritual in my house.
Open 'til 12 Fri-Sat. 11 rest of the week.

Fortune Wheel
151 Mansfield Road (0115) 924 0639
Open 'til 12.

Saigon
72 Trent Road (0115) 950 4616
Open 'til 12.30. Closed Tuesdays.
Delivery service.

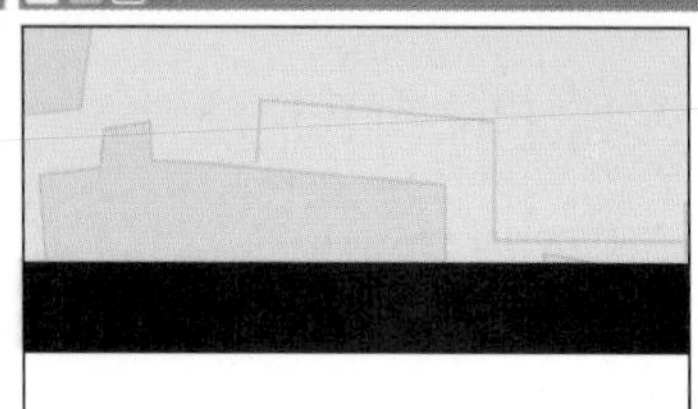

laters

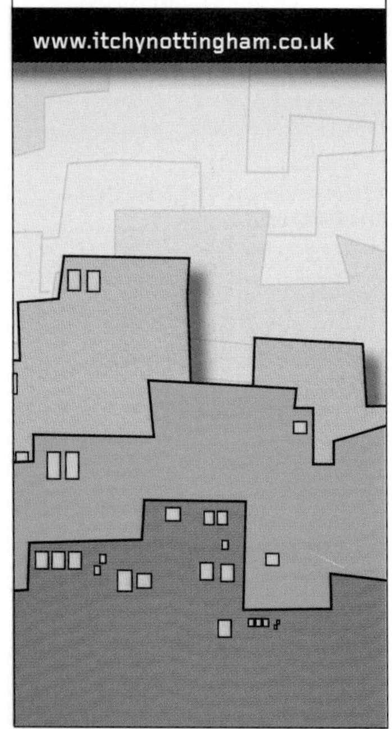

Late night drinking

Thankfully the number of late bars is on the up. Pick of the bunch is **The Social**: open 'til 1am most nights, 2am Friday and Saturday. **Bar None's** open until 2am and is free on Thursday and Friday, and you can drink away 'til 1am at **Sugar Bar** and **Bluu**.

Cigarettes at 4am?

24 hour garage on Huntingdon Street is probably the most central place to quell that craving when Nick O'Teen starts whispering in your ear at 4am.

After hours fridge stocking

Alldays on Bridgford road in West Bridgford is open 24 hours a day 365 days a year, making it the ultimate place for stocking up on muffins and milkshakes if you've got those inexplicable late munchies we all get from time to time.

Food now

Pizza Stop Number 5 on Mansfield Road is probably the latest place that'll deliver you a chicken tikka kebab. They keep plugging away until about 4am meaning that the biggest problem is the likelyhood of falling asleep/passing out before they get to you. They're not best pleased when you do this, and repeat offending will lead to blacklisting, as I have unfortunately found out.

Nice food now!

Joking aren't you. **Sapna's** is about the latest seating restaurant in town, but it's hardly Gordon Ramsey at the helm.

Post club action

I never get invited to after club parties, so there better bleeding not be any.

Late-night shopping

Things vary seasonally but like most cities, Thursday is generally the night most likely for late night opening.

top 5 for...
late drinking

1. The Social
2. Bluu
3. Sugar Bar
4. Brass Monkey
5. Wax

Still not tired?

The true dirty stop out, or those in lumber with their other halves can find the ultimate late night refuge at **Rileys Snooker Club** on St James. Open 24-7 you could in theory move in. The membership's certainly a lot cheaper than city centre rent these days and the hustle potential means you could make quite a tasty living.

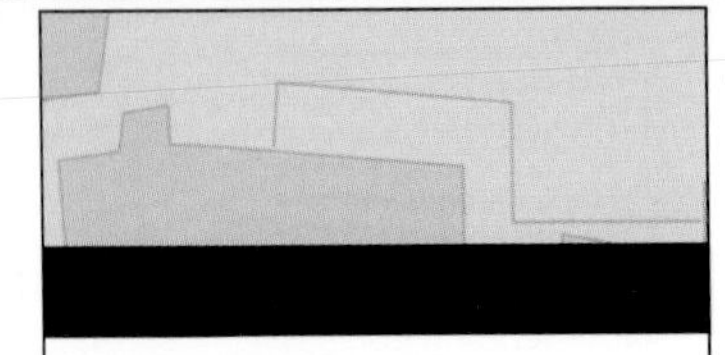

useful info

www.itchynottingham.co.uk

Airport

East Midlands Airport
Castle Donnington Airport, Derby
..........(01332) 852852

Nottingham Airport
Tollerton Airport, Tollerton Lane
..........(0115) 981 1327

Public Transport

Traveline
Public transport hotline
..........0870 608 2608

Bus and Coach

National Express
Broad Marsh Bus Station
..........08705 808 080

Nottingham City Transport
Lower Parliament Street
..........(0115) 950 5745

Nottingham Bus Hotline
..........08706 082 608

Rail

National Rail Enquiries
..........08457 484 950

Taxis

I'm afraid there's no secret trick to flagging a cab after slinging out time, but here's a couple of words of wisdom you might want to heed. Biting the bullet and actually joining the queues at the Market Square or Victoria

Centre ranks is probably the fastest way of getting home, but never seems a good idea after a night on the falling down water. The queues at the train station rank are usually shorter, and it'll save you a quid or so if you're heading to the Meadows or West Bridgford, but it's obviously false economy if you're only going back into town to head north of the city. We of course wouldn't condone flagging down cabs on the street, especially around Weekday Cross and Listergate (as that's my spot) so good luck out there.

A1 Cars ....(0115) 9708708
A2B ....(0115) 9708090
Apex Cars ....(0115) 9642007
ATA City Cabs ....(0115) 9701701
Cable Cars ....(0115) 9229229
DG Cars ....(0115) 9607607
Sky Cars ....(0115) 9145145
Trent Cars ....(0115) 9505050
Yellow Cars ....(0115) 9818181

Car Hire

Arriva
London Road
....(0115) 955 744/955 7400

Avis
The Arndale Centre, Maid Marion Way
....(0115) 950 1872

Hertz
Bath Place, Bath Street
....(0115) 958 0575

National Car Rental
Mabel Street
....0870 400 4502

Accommodation

Luxury

Holiday Inn

Castle Marina Park, Lenton
(0115) 993 5000
Handily placed for trips to Sainsburys.
Double rooms: £92 all week

Lace Market Hotel

29 Pavement Street (0115) 852 3232
Good on-site restaurant and a host of near-by bars.
Single rooms: £89 weekdays,
£69 weekends

Waltons Hotel

2 North Road
(0115) 947 5215
Popular for functions and parties.
Single room: £75 all week

Medium

Comfort Hotel

George Street, (0115) 947 5641
Bang in the heart of Hockley.
Double rooms: £65 weekday
£40 weekends

Langar Hall Hotel

Langar Hall, Langar (0194) 986 0559
Excellent restaurant.
Single room from £65

Strathdon Thistle Hotel

Derby Road (0115) 941 8501
Single room: £68 Weekdays
£39 Weekends.

Budget

The Beeches

Wilford Lane, West Bridgeford
(0115) 981 8753
Single room: £59 Weekdays
£38 Weekends

Bentink Hotel

Station Street (0115) 958 0285
Right next to the train station the bar gets full of football fans on match days.
Single room: £20 all week

Media

General publications

itchy Nottingham – F'ing ace, you should buy it. Oh you have. Cool.
City Lights – Useful monthly listings mag.
69 – Some useful Nottingham information amongst lots of stories about being hip and hedonistic and talking to DJs and doing all the things that I'd do if only I was as cool as them.
What's On – Council produced monthly guide. A page-turner it aint, but it is very informative and factually accurate.
Hair of the Dog – Annually published guide to Nottingham socialising produced in conjunction with the council and the Nottingham Post Group.

Radio

96 Trent FM – Primarily pop.
Century 106fm – Travis FM during the day, the real gem in centuries crown is 'Fletch and Birtles' football phone-in which runs from 6-8pm weeknights and is unmissable for all East Midlands football fans.

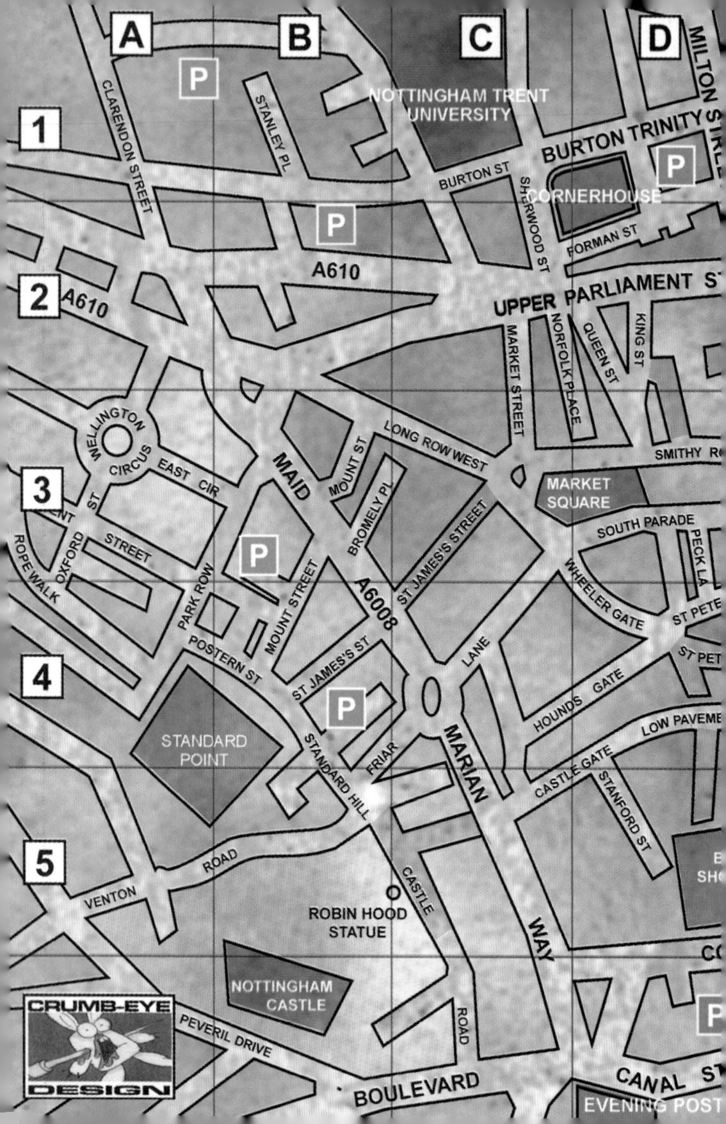

A
B
C
D
1
2
3
4
5
CLARENDON STREET
STANLEY PL
NOTTINGHAM TRENT UNIVERSITY
BURTON ST
SHERWOOD ST
BURTON TRINITY
CORNERHOUSE
FORMAN ST
A610
UPPER PARLIAMENT
MARKET STREET
NORFOLK PLACE
QUEEN ST
KING ST
WELLINGTON CIRCUS
EAST CIR
MAID
MOUNT ST
LONG ROW WEST
BROMELY PL
MARKET SQUARE
SOUTH PARADE
ST
OXFORD
STREET
ROPE WALK
PARK ROW
MOUNT STREET
A6008
ST JAMES'S STREET
WHEELER GATE
POSTERN ST
ST JAMES'S ST
LANE
HOUNDS GATE
STANDARD POINT
STANDARD HILL
FRIAR
MARIAN
CASTLE GATE
STANFORD ST
ROAD
VENTON
CASTLE
ROBIN HOOD STATUE
WAY
NOTTINGHAM CASTLE
CRUMB-EYE DESIGN
PEVERIL DRIVE
ROAD
BOULEVARD
CANAL

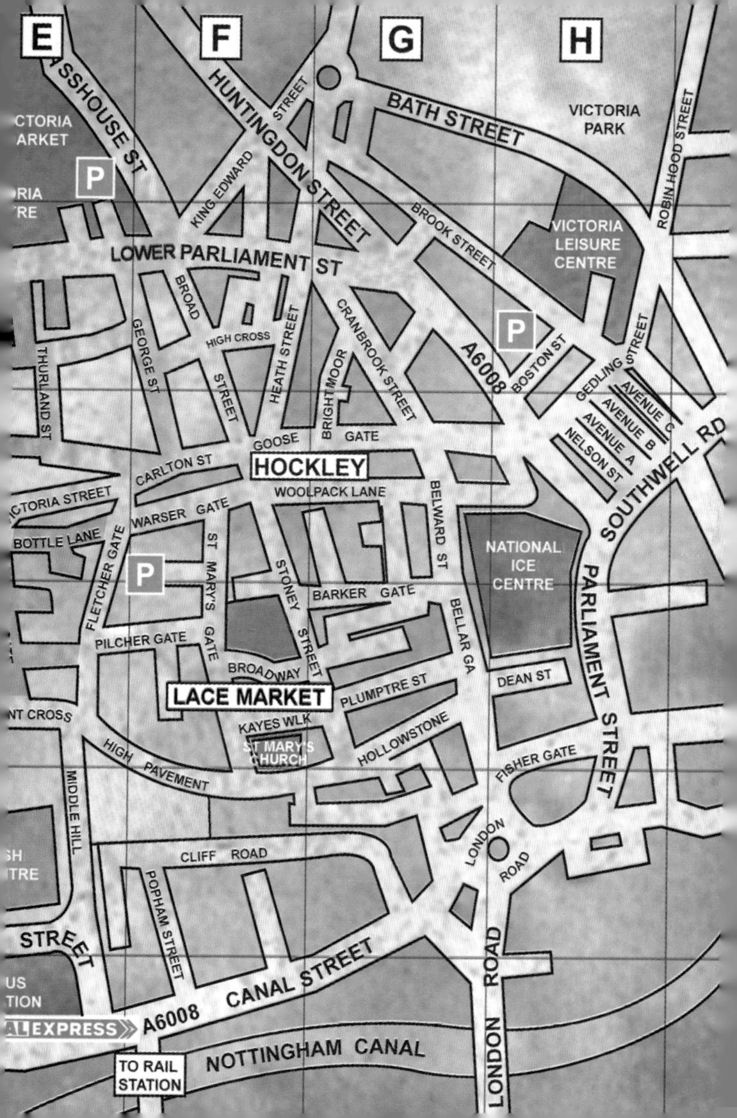
E
F
G
H
HUNTINGDON STREET
STREET
BATH STREET
VICTORIA PARK
ROBIN HOOD STREET
KING EDWARD
BROOK STREET
VICTORIA LEISURE CENTRE
LOWER PARLIAMENT ST
BROAD
GEORGE ST
HIGH CROSS
HEATH STREET
CRANBROOK STREET
BRIGHTMOOR
A6008
BOSTON ST
GEDLING STREET
AVENUE C
AVENUE B
AVENUE A
NELSON ST
THURLAND ST
STREET
GOOSE
GATE
HOCKLEY
CARLTON ST
WOOLPACK LANE
BELWARD ST
SOUTHWELL RD
WARSER GATE
BOTTLE LANE
FLETCHER GATE
ST MARY'S GATE
STONEY STREET
BARKER GATE
NATIONAL ICE CENTRE
PARLIAMENT STREET
BELLAR GA
PILCHER GATE
BROADWAY
PLUMPTRE ST
DEAN ST
LACE MARKET
KAYES WLK
ST MARY'S CHURCH
HOLLOWSTONE
HIGH PAVEMENT
FISHER GATE
MIDDLE HILL
LONDON ROAD
CLIFF ROAD
POPHAM STREET
STREET
CANAL STREET
A6008
EXPRESS
NOTTINGHAM CANAL
TO RAIL STATION
LONDON ROAD

index

Oh my God we're good to you...

Not only do we write funky little books but we also offer you, the discerning entertainment junkie, some pretty fine stuff on-line.

Point your browser to **www.itchycity.co.uk** and we'll not only keep you entertained with stories and reviews about what's going on in your city, we can also send you regular emails and SMS messages about the stuff you're into. So, we'll keep you informed about where the best happy hours are, when Oakenfold's next in town or where you can find a kebab at 2am. There's also a chance for you to contribute your views and reviews and get free stuff in return (we are too good to you). Have a shoofty. Go on.

Go to www.itchynottingham.co.uk, click on itchyme, and sign up for:

Cheap Drinks / offers • Cheap Eats / offers • House & Garage • Techno & Electronica • Jazz, Soul, Reggae & Funk • Indie • Metal & Alternative • Hip Hop, R'n'B & Breaks • Drum n' Bass & Jungle • Sixties, Northern Soul & Motown • Seventies, Eighties & Disco • Pop & Rock • Classical & Opera • World, Folk and Latin • Gay • Comedy • Stage • Art • And all the venues we feature in the book

itchy box set

Oh, imagine. **All 16 titles**, an encyclopaedia of entertainment across the country, all wrapped up in a glorious multi-coloured special box. Every title below in one mother of a box. Limited edition, naturally, and so exclusive, we don't even know what it looks like ourselves.

Artist's impression. Is this what the box will look like?

If you were to buy these individually, it'd cost you a bargainous £44. But hello, what's this? We're doing the full caboodle **for a mere £35**, including free postage and packing. **Call 0113 246 0440** and order by credit/debit card and we'll whizz one over to you.

bath birmingham brighton bristol cambridge cardiff edinburgh glasgow leeds liverpool london manchester nottingham oxford sheffield york

THEY MUST PROMOTE
YOU. YOU'VE GOT
COMMITMENT.
BEWARE OF THE VOICES. FOR CAREER ADVICE WORTH LISTENING TO
AND THOUSANDS OF JOBS, VISIT
monster.co.uk